YOU CAN LEARN!

Building Student Ownership, Motivation, and Efficacy With the PLC at Work® Process

TIM BROWN & WILLIAM M. FERRITER

Solution Tree | Press

a division of
Solution Tree

555 North Morton Street
Bloomington, IN 47404
800.733.6786 (toll free) / 812.336.7700
FAX: 812.336.7790

email: info@SolutionTree.com
SolutionTree.com

Visit **go.SolutionTree.com/PLCbooks** to download the free reproducibles in this book.

Printed in the United States of America

Library of Congress Cataloging-in-Publication Data

Names: Brown, Tim, 1956- author. | Ferriter, William M., author.
Title: You can learn! : building student ownership, motivation, and
    efficacy with the PLC at work® process / Tim Brown, William M. Ferriter.

Description: Bloomington, IN : Solution Tree Press, 2021. | Includes
    bibliographical references and index.
Identifiers: LCCN 2021017065 (print) | LCCN 2021017066 (ebook) | ISBN
    9781952812491 (paperback) | ISBN 9781952812507 (ebook)
Subjects: LCSH: Motivation in education. | Academic achievement. |
    Self-efficacy. | Professional learning communities.
Classification: LCC LB1065 .B7794 2021 (print) | LCC LB1065 (ebook) | DDC
    370.15/4--dc23
LC record available at https://lccn.loc.gov/2021017065
LC ebook record available at https://lccn.loc.gov/2021017066

Solution Tree
Jeffrey C. Jones, CEO
Edmund M. Ackerman, President

Solution Tree Press
President and Publisher: Douglas M. Rife
Associate Publisher: Sarah Payne-Mills
Art Director: Rian Anderson
Managing Production Editor: Kendra Slayton
Copy Chief: Jessi Finn
Senior Production Editor: Suzanne Kraszewski
Content Development Specialist: Amy Rubenstein
Copy Editor: Kate St. Ives
Proofreader: Elisabeth Abrams
Text and Cover Designer: Abigail Bowen
Editorial Assistants: Sarah Ludwig and Elijah Oates

ACKNOWLEDGMENTS

We never go it alone in the complex world of teaching and learning. As such, I would like to dedicate this book to my wife, Donna, who has encouraged my journey as an educator every step of the way. Without her coaxing, support, and bribery this book may never have been written. I'd also like to raise a glass and give a shout-out to my children: Miles, Adam, Katherine, and Madeline, who along with their children bolstered my drive to share these ideas in writing. It is my hope that every educator my grandchildren have will incorporate the practices this book supports.

I would also like to express my gratitude to my associates in this work, and the educators who have willingly shared their examples from the field with me. A huge thanks goes to my coauthor, Bill Ferriter, who shows a deep understanding of the impact of these practices because he uses them every day with his middle school students. Finally, a special thanks to Bob Eaker who asked me some time ago if I had seen the research on teaching vicariously, through the eyes of the student; this led me to the first of many "Ah-has," "Amens," and "So what?"s.

—Tim Brown

This book is dedicated to my daughter, Reece, who inspires me to be both a better teacher and father every single day, and to the teachers she has yet to have. I would also like to thank the entire team at Solution Tree Press for the time and energy that they have invested into bringing this book to life. Finally, I would like to acknowledge Rick DuFour and Bob Eaker, whose thinking on just what learning for the adults in a schoolhouse should look like has forever changed my professional life as a classroom teacher for the better, and Becky DuFour, whose belief in the power of my voice and the value of my experience continues to resonate inside of me even today.

—Bill Ferriter

Solution Tree Press would like to thank the following reviewers:

Molly Capps
Principal
McDeeds Creek Elementary
Southern Pines, North Carolina

Scott Hagerman
Superintendent
Tanque Verde USD
Tucson, Arizona

Maria Krum
Special Education Teacher
Los Lunas Elementary
Los Lunas, New Mexico

Katie Madigan
Principal
Glasgow Middle School
Alexandria, Virginia

Bo Ryan
Principal
Greater Hartford Academy of the
  Arts Middle School
Hartford, Connecticut

Claire Springer
Assistant Principal
Savannah Elementary School
Denton, Texas

Jennifer Steele
Assistant Principal
Northside High School
Fort Smith, Arkansas

Emily Terry
English Teacher
Kinard Middle School
Fort Collins, Colorado

Kim Timmerman
Principal
Adel DeSoto Minburn Middle School
Adel, Iowa

Visit **go.SolutionTree.com/PLCbooks** to download the free reproducibles in this book.

TABLE OF CONTENTS

Reproducible pages are in italics.

CHAPTER 4

Helping Students Take Action. **81**

ABOUT THE AUTHORS

Tim Brown, EdS, is a veteran educator from Springfield, Missouri. As a building principal, Tim engaged his staff in the Professional Learning Communities at Work® process to create a culture of high expectations for all students. The schools he led saw dramatic increases in student achievement through their collaborative efforts. His middle school was celebrated as a Missouri Top Ten Gold Star School. His last school, a high poverty elementary school, was recognized as Missouri's Most Improved School and an Exemplary Practices School. In 2005, Tim was honored by his peers as Missouri's Distinguished Elementary Principal.

After retiring from Springfield Public Schools, Tim became the director of professional learning communities for the Heart of Missouri Regional Professional Development Center. As an associate with Solution Tree, he worked closely with Richard DuFour and Rebecca DuFour, and continues to work with Robert Eaker. For the past several years, Tim has been developing professional learning materials and conducting trainings around the globe that help educators create a culture of learning within their schools. His keynotes, workshops, trainings, and consulting work are characterized as highly engaging and practical. Participants in his workshops leave motivated and equipped for high levels of collaboration that result in increases in student achievement.

Tim earned his bachelor's degree from the University of Central Arkansas. He holds a master's and specialist degree from Missouri State University.

To learn more about Tim, follow him @ctimbrown on Twitter.

William M. Ferriter, MS, is an eighth-grade science teacher in a PLC near Raleigh, North Carolina. A National Board Certified Teacher for the past twenty-five years, Bill has designed professional development courses for educators nationwide on topics ranging from establishing PLCs and using technology to reimagining learning spaces to integrating meaningful student-involved assessment and feedback opportunities into classroom instruction.

What Bill brings to audiences is practical experience gained through extensive and continuing work with his own professional learning team and students in his classroom. Teachers appreciate the practicality of both his writing and his presentations, knowing that the content shared is content that is currently being used by a full-time classroom teacher. Every book that he writes and session that he delivers is designed to give participants not just a clear understanding of the whys behind the ideas that he is introducing, but tangible examples of how to turn those ideas into classroom and collaborative practices that work.

Bill has had articles published in *Phi Delta Kappan* magazine, *Journal of Staff Development*, *Educational Leadership*, and *Threshold Magazine*. A contributing author to two assessment anthologies, *The Teacher as Assessment Leader* and *The Principal as Assessment Leader*, he is also coauthor of several books, including *Teaching the iGeneration, Building a Professional Learning Community at Work*®, *Making Teamwork Meaningful*, and *Creating a Culture of Feedback*.

Bill earned a bachelor of science and master of science in elementary education from the State University of New York at Geneseo.

To learn more about Bill's work, visit his blog The Tempered Radical (http://blog.williamferriter .com) or follow @plugusin on Twitter.

To book Tim Brown or William M. Ferriter for professional development, contact pd@SolutionTree.com.

Introduction

Think for a minute about the full range of academic behaviors on display in your classroom each day. Odds are that you have some students who raise their hand every time you ask a question, excited to share their thoughts, while others sit passively in the back, never volunteering to contribute. Some take the lead on group projects, making suggestions and setting direction for their peers, while others rarely contribute ideas that move the work forward. Some lean into every homework assignment, consistently exceeding grade-level expectations and producing "hang it on the wall work," while others consistently show up on your list for missing tasks.

What explains these differences? Why do some students become enthusiastic learners while others seem to give up?

The answer lies in the experiences that students have in our schools. Enthusiastic learners have experienced success time and again. They regularly earn the best marks on tests and quizzes. They are always at the top of class rankings. They place in the highest percentiles of standardized tests year after year. As a result, they *believe* in their academic abilities. That belief inspires their participation, carries them through moments when learning is hard, and increases their willingness to take intellectual risks. It is easy to be confident, after all, when you see consistent evidence that you are competent.

Students who have given up, however, rarely see *any* evidence that they can be successful in school. Years of struggle—low marks on quizzes and tests, frustration with tasks that other students seem to complete with ease, confusion with concepts introduced in daily lessons—have left these learners *skeptical* of their own academic abilities. As a result, struggling students use avoidance as a coping strategy in any situation where they expect to fail (Wolf, 2007). As Angela Duckworth (2020), professor at the University of Pennsylvania and expert on the role that grit plays in successful learning, explains:

> The main idea is simple: if you attempt hard things, again and again, and eventually succeed, you come to believe in your capabilities. In contrast, if you fail repeatedly, you come to believe that you can't succeed, even if you try.

There is nothing surprising here, right? Learners who believe in their own ability to "produce desired effects and forestall undesired ones"(Bandura, 2009, Location No. 4919)—a trait that Albert Bandura (2009) calls *self-efficacy*—are successful because they are more likely to persist through academic challenge. Learners who are not convinced that they can be successful rarely demonstrate the persistence and motivation necessary to achieve at the highest levels (Bandura, 2009; Hattie & Clarke, 2019).

What may surprise you is just how important self-efficacy is for learners. High levels of self-efficacy can enhance a student's accomplishments, feelings of personal well-being, and willingness to experiment with new ideas. Students with high levels of self-efficacy also set higher expectations for their future performance and remain calm when approaching difficult tasks (Bandura, 2009; Hattie & Clarke, 2019; Ormrod, 2008; Pajares, 1997). And perhaps most important, self-efficacy has a positive impact on a student's academic achievement. Its .71 effect size translates to a 26-percentile-point gain, making self-efficacy one of the most effective instructional strategies that teachers can implement in their classrooms (Hattie, 2018). Helping students to develop a stronger sense of self-efficacy—which John Hattie (2009) describes as "gaining a reputation as a learner" (Location No. 2464) may even have a greater impact on learning than addressing achievement directly.

About This Book

You Can Learn! Building Student Ownership, Motivation, and Efficacy With the PLC at Work Process is designed to introduce readers to the intentional and purposeful steps they can take to increase the self-efficacy of every learner. Each chapter introduces research in the field of efficacy advanced by experts including Albert Bandura, John Hattie, Shirley Clarke, Robert Marzano, Jan Chappuis, Susan Brookhart, Carol Dweck, Dylan Wiliam, and Rick Stiggins. Readers will also learn how the core concepts of that research can be translated into specific instructional practices designed to direct and elicit greater student engagement and ownership of learning. Finally, each chapter includes exemplars of efficacy-building practices that are currently in use in classrooms that cross multiple grade levels and subject areas. These exemplars—paired with their corresponding protocols and instructional materials—are designed to serve as inspiration for readers, proving that efficacy-building really can become an important part of the work that we do with students.

What makes this book unique in the canon of literature of self-efficacy is that we draw clear parallels between the collective efficacy-building behaviors of collaborative teams and the actions students who demonstrate high levels of efficacy take. Readers will learn about the role that student-led mission, vision, values, and goals statements—core elements in the foundation of any Professional Learning Community at Work (PLC at Work)—can play in establishing and reinforcing a culture of learning in classrooms. Readers will also learn about how the four critical questions of a PLC—"What knowledge, skills, and dispositions should every student acquire as a result of this unit, this course, or this grade level? How will we know when each student has acquired the essential knowledge and

skills? How will we respond if students do not learn? and How will we extend learning for students who are already proficient?" (DuFour, DuFour, Eaker, Many, & Mattos, 2016, p. 36)—can be adapted for use as a part of any effort to build the academic confidence and competence of learners.

In addition to an introduction and a conclusion, this book includes four chapters with titles that will sound familiar to practitioners well-versed in PLC at Work concepts and behaviors.

Chapter 1: Building a Commitment to Learning in Students

In a PLC at Work, mission, vision, values, and goals statements are used to build a shared commitment to learning between members of a school's faculty. Known as the *four pillars of a PLC* (DuFour et al., 2016), mission, vision, values, and goals statements detail the central beliefs of a school or district and outline the core behaviors everyone is expected to live up to. More important, they become a tool to motivate, inspire, and drive all faculty members forward. Teachers working to increase the levels of efficacy in their students can use the development of promise statements, classroom norms, and classroom success walls to build the same kind of commitment to learning in their classrooms. This chapter will introduce readers to strategies for how to do this.

Chapter 2: Helping Students Understand the Expectations for a Unit of Study

Collaborative teams start each cycle of collective inquiry by answering the first critical question of a PLC (DuFour et al., 2016): What knowledge, skills, and dispositions should every student acquire as a result of this unit? Answering this question together helps teachers to identify a small set of outcomes that are essential for every student to learn. Teachers working to increase the levels of efficacy in their students then take active steps to communicate those expectations in their classrooms. This chapter introduces readers to the role that relevance statements, success checklists, and exemplars can play in helping students to better understand just what they are supposed to learn during a unit of study.

Chapter 3: Helping Students Assess Their Progress Toward Mastery

Once collaborative teams have identified a small handful of essential outcomes for a cycle of inquiry, they answer the second critical question of a PLC (DuFour et al., 2016)—How will we know when each student has learned the content, skills, or behaviors that we have identified as essential?—by developing a plan for assessing learning. Progress toward mastery is tracked by both student and standard, giving teachers information that they can use to act on behalf of students. Teachers working to increase the levels of efficacy in their students recognize, however, that giving learners regular opportunities *to gather evidence of their own progress* is the best way to develop academic confidence. This chapter shows readers how they can integrate simple student self-assessment strategies like student planning, goal setting, and progress tracking into their instruction.

Chapter 4: Helping Students Take Action

After collaborative teams have collected information from assessments, they answer the third and fourth critical questions of learning in a PLC at Work (DuFour et al., 2016): How will we respond if students do not learn? and How will we extend learning for students who are already proficient? Teams plan and deliver customized support for students who need additional instruction, extra practice, or extension, knowing that just-in-time intervention is the best way to help every learner experience success. Teachers working to increase the levels of efficacy in their students understand that using information to plan next steps is a specific behavior that can be introduced to learners. Without guidance from educators, a student can easily misinterpret his or her results on an assignment or assessment. The feeling that comes from a student thinking, "I'm not very good at this" is a key influencer on one's efficacy judgement (Hattie & Clarke, 2019). This chapter introduces readers to test trackers, assessment wrappers, next-step checklists, and six-week grade check-ins—simple tools that students can use to make immediate adjustments to the course of their own learning during a unit of instruction.

While the content included in this book is intentionally organized around the foundational practices of collaborative teams in a PLC at Work (DuFour et al., 2016), and while those practices are intentionally designed to be completed sequentially, there is no one right way to read this book. If you are new to collaboration or to the kinds of steps that teachers take to build self-efficacy in students, you might choose to read this book from cover to cover. Doing so will give you a structured sense of both the core work of collaborative teams in a PLC and the role that same work can play in developing self-efficacious learners. If you have a solid understanding of the core work of collaborative teams in PLCs and you have already begun experimenting with asking students to engage in similar cycles of collective inquiry around their own learning, turn this book into a toolkit that you can draw from on an as-needed basis. The table of contents—which identifies both the content each chapter covers as well as the strategies we recommend for turning the collaborative processes teacher teams use in PLCs into instructional practices used with students—can help you identify logical starting points for your work within this text.

There is also no one right audience for this book because all students—regardless of their grade level, life circumstances, or learning context—deserve to see themselves as capable and competent learners. While we would argue that integrating self-efficacy practices into the elementary classroom can have the greatest long-term impact on both learners and schools, older students are often the most in need of evidence of their ability to succeed academically. As you will learn later in this text, research on high school dropouts (Feldman, Smith, & Waxman, 2017) shows that struggling students often first lose confidence in middle grades classrooms—places where tweens and teens are wrestling with their own independence and identity while simultaneously working in spaces where lessons move at a faster pace and where the high stakes of failure become evident to everyone. And high school is our last opportunity as teachers to leave our students with the skills necessary to effectively respond to any circumstance that they may face moving forward into their adult lives. If we allow high schoolers to leave our buildings unsure of just how to identify and then close the gap between *where they are* and *where they most want to be*, there is little chance that they will reach their fullest potential in the increasingly complex and unpredictable world that we are living in.

But there are some students who depend on our efforts to integrate self-efficacy practices into our instruction more than others—students in poor, urban communities and students who are learning remotely. Students in poor, urban communities often experience a completely different education than their counterparts living in middle- and upper-class neighborhoods. Systemically, school funding in poor, urban communities "is on average, 30 percent less than suburban schools that serve primarily white, middle-class students" (Muhammad, 2017, Location No. 357). Those schools are also less likely to offer courses in advanced sciences or mathematics, less likely to have high percentages of students enrolled in academically gifted programs, and less likely to have high numbers of experienced teachers (Muhammad, 2017).

Worse yet are the perceptions that some educators hold of students living in poor, urban communities. They are often seen first for their weaknesses instead of their strengths, labeled as "low achievers" or "minorities" coming from "disadvantaged communities" (Jackson, 2011, p. 41). As a result of these pervasive labels, their capacity for learning at the highest levels is doubted by the system designed to serve them, and their schooling is often stripped of challenge and centered on remediation (Jackson, 2011). As Yvette Jackson (2011) explains, this "myth of weakness" that surrounds students from poor, urban communities causes us to "turn our backs on the vast intellectual capacity of these students and to regard minimum proficiency as the ceiling" (p. 20).

Classroom teachers and school leaders may not be able to address all the systemic inequities that students from poor, urban communities face, but we can teach our students the skills necessary to *identify and develop their own strengths*. Students who can identify and develop their own strengths experience "confidence acquired from competence" (Jackson, 2011, p. 32) again and again, quickly learning that they can succeed in any circumstance. That makes the strategies introduced in this book even more important for teachers

working with students who are the most dependent on schools for advancing their opportunities.

Students who are learning remotely—a trend likely to grow in the years following school interruptions due to the COVID-19 pandemic—are also more dependent on our efforts to integrate self-efficacy practices into our instruction. Here is why: students who are learning remotely lose out on the tacit feedback provided by the environment in face-to-face classrooms. They can't quickly glance at a peer's paper to see how their work measures up. They can't automatically listen in on the questions asked of the teacher by other students and see if they know the answer. They can't easily read the temperature of their classroom to see if the academic tension that they are feeling in moments of challenge is also felt by their peers. Absent those informal cues, students learning remotely often question both themselves and their performances more than students learning in face-to-face environments. That makes the ability to self-assess even more important for students who are, for the most part, learning alone (Ferriter, 2020).

The good news is that integrating self-efficacy into our instructional practices looks the same for teachers working with students in poor, urban communities and in remote learning environments as it does for teachers who are working in face-to-face classrooms with students in suburban schools. The core behaviors of self-efficacious learners—accurately identifying strengths and weaknesses in your own work, spotting places where you are making progress, and choosing next steps worth taking—are not context dependent. Sure, teachers working with students learning remotely will have to find digital methods to share the tools in this text with their students based on the unique platforms and technologies that their districts are using, but the core principles and practices introduced in the following four chapters remain relevant no matter what your teaching circumstances look like. That means *every teacher* and *every principal* and every *instructional coach* can learn from this book. If you care most about primary classrooms, you might be interested in the work being done by the teachers at Mason Crest Elementary School, who are using primary progress tracking cards (chapter 3), for example, to teach their youngest learners to keep records of the progress that they are making at mastering important outcomes. If you care most about middle grades classrooms, you might be interested in the work being done by Paul Cancellieri, who uses exemplars and single-point rubrics (chapter 2) to help students better understand the expectations for important assignments and to better evaluate their own final products. And if you care most about high school classrooms, you might be interested in the work being done by the teachers at Fern Creek High School in Louisville, who guide their students through "six-week grade check-ins" (chapter 4) that are carefully designed to turn *grades earned* into *information that students can act on* to improve their own performance. *You Can Learn!* is filled with examples that highlight the strategies teachers across the K–12 spectrum are using to integrate student self-efficacy into their instruction.

Concluding Thoughts

Since the early 2000s, researchers (Bandura, 2009; Hattie & Clarke, 2019; Hattie, 2009; Wolf, 2007) have proven that self-efficacy "can be measured, can be influenced, and most importantly, correlates with the actual probability of success in tasks that require motivation and persistence" (Wolf, 2007). Our hope is that this book will help teams to positively influence the key factors that impact a student's efficacy judgements—and by doing so, increase the probability of success of every student in their care.

1 Building a Commitment to Learning in Students

Tim Brown, coauthor of this book, once served as the principal of Campbell Elementary School in Springfield, Missouri. As principal, Tim started every school year with what he called a "challenge assembly." Challenge assemblies, built around the theme the faculty set for the year, were designed to reinforce the school's mission, vision, values, and goals. Tim's favorite challenge assembly theme was "Let's Build a Brighter Tomorrow Together, One Brick at a Time." On the first day of the school year, Tim showed up to the challenge assembly dressed in a hard hat and wearing a tool belt. He went on to introduce the yearly theme to both the staff and students using a modified version of the opening music to the Bob the Builder children's television show that included both the name and mascot of the school. Some of the lyrics follow.

> Campbell Cougars, can we build it?
> Campbell Cougars, yes we can!
> We are the Cougars, and we are the best.
> We are the Cougars, and we won't rest.
> Working together we get learning done.
> Working together we make learning fun.
> Campbell Cougars, can we build it?
> Campbell Cougars, YES WE CAN!

When they finished singing, Tim asked the student body to think about the things that a builder would need to create a solid structure. After taking several answers from students, such as *tools, wood, windows,* and *workers*, Tim shared that one of the first things a builder needs is a *vision* of what the project will look like when it is finished. "If you aren't sure of what your final structure is going to look like *before* you start building," he reminded the students, "you won't be able to make the right plans or take the right steps to make your vision become a reality."

Tim then shared his vision of what Campbell Elementary would look like by the end of the year. He wanted everyone in the community—parents, visitors, substitute teachers—to see Campbell Elementary as a school with high expectations that provides a respectful environment for all students. That was a commitment that both he and his teachers were willing to make to their students.

Tim went on to explain that he also wanted Campbell Elementary to be known as a school that changed lives. In a school that changes lives, he explained, teachers design lessons that help students master essential outcomes and work to ensure that every student feels recognized and appreciated. In a school that changes lives, students lean into every lesson, giving their best effort no matter how challenging new tasks and content seem. They also go out of their way to show empathy and support to their peers. Finally, in a school that changes lives, parents, principals, and paraprofessionals do all they can to support student learning. They keep everyone safe, make sure everyone has the supplies needed to learn at the highest levels, and solve all the little problems that come up daily in the building. Each of these actions, Tim explained, are like the bricks in their building—providing structure for their efforts to change lives—and everyone in the school's community could contribute to their school's goal by following through on their promises to one another each and every day.

He finished the assembly, like every other assembly in previous years, by having both students and teachers participate in the following Cougar Pledge.

> I will face the challenges before me.
>
> I will not run and hide.
>
> I know my teachers love me.
>
> They will always be by my side.
>
> But when it comes to my success,
>
> There are things that I must do.
>
> I must think, act, and show that I can handle anything new.
>
> Cougar CLAWS will always guide me.
>
> No more working to just get by.
>
> I will have Courage to Learn, Achieve, Win, and Succeed.
>
> And I will hold these CLAWS up high.
>
> Because when it comes to my success,
>
> There are things that I must do.
>
> I must think, act, and show that I can handle anything new.
>
> When I walk through these doors every day,
>
> My work will be done with pride.
>
> I will listen to what others have to say,
>
> And my dreams will not be denied.
>
> Because when it comes down to my success,
>
> There are things that I must do.
>
> I must think, act, and show that I can handle anything new.
>
> I WILL think, act, and show that I can handle anything new!

The building theme continued throughout the year at Campbell Elementary. To reconnect students to the purpose of the school, Tim held weekly challenge assemblies first thing every Monday morning. For Tim, those weekly assemblies were essential because they gave students the chance to see the role that they play in moving the mission and the vision of the school forward. What is more, weekly challenge assemblies turned affirmation of values and beliefs of the building into more than a one-time event. Each assembly became a platform to communicate the school's expectations; to reinforce the school's mission, vision, values, and goals; to celebrate with one another; and to develop a sense of unity across the entire building.

Throughout the year, students who had contributed to the goals of the school were recognized with yellow plastic hard hats that they could wear to weekly challenge assemblies. Students also received construction paper bricks with their names printed on them each time they took a step—showing determination in the face of challenge, extending support to a struggling classmate, demonstrating mastery on a classroom assessment—that moved the school forward. Those bricks were collected at challenge assemblies and then placed on a large bulletin board in the main hallway of the school. Eventually, the bulletin board was filled with hundreds of bricks, and the assemblies became a sea of yellow hard hats. Those bricks and hard hats served as a visual reminder for the entire school community that by working together, Campbell Elementary students and staff really *could* create a brighter tomorrow, one brick at a time.

Why Is This Important to Learners?

In his seminal book *Good to Great*, organizational theorist Jim Collins (2001) makes a simple claim: The most successful companies always have a big, hairy, audacious goal (BHAG). To Collins (2001), a BHAG is "a huge and daunting goal—like a big mountain to climb. It is clear, compelling, and people get it right away. It serves as a unifying focal point of effort, galvanizing people and creating team spirit as people strive towards a finish line" (p. 202). President John F. Kennedy understood the inspirational power of BHAGs. He issued one on September 12, 1962, announcing that America would land a man on the moon by the end of the decade. That goal captured the imagination of the American people and pushed an entire nation to new heights together (Collins, 2001).

In the story that starts this chapter, author and building principal Tim Brown issued his own BHAG for Campbell Elementary: *We are going to build a brighter tomorrow, one brick at a time.* This simple statement became a powerful tool for motivating Tim's school community. It provided a grounding point for decisions that kept Campbell Elementary moving in the right direction. It also became something that everyone in the Campbell Elementary community could relate to, identify with, and promote as their primary purpose. Why did teachers work hard to know students as individuals at Campbell Elementary? Why did students lean in on challenging assignments at Campbell Elementary? Why did support personnel work hard to create the conditions necessary for students to succeed at Campbell Elementary? It was not just because they wanted a yellow hard hat and a construction paper brick. It was because they knew that doing so would help to build a brighter tomorrow—and the idea of building a brighter tomorrow together galvanized the entire Campbell community. They wanted to be a part of something bigger than themselves.

In many ways, schools functioning as PLCs use their mission, vision, values, and goals in the same way that successful businesses use BHAGs. Knowing why we exist (mission), describing what we want to become (vision), locking down our commitments (values), and focusing on the objective of all students learning at high levels (goals) can inspire us on tough days, move us to higher levels of performance, and renew our spirit. These foundational blocks—what DuFour and colleagues (2016) call pillars—can become a catalyst for necessary conversations that lead to greater effort and renewed service. They can also challenge us and serve as a call to action. Leaders use them throughout the year to reconnect their faculties to the primary purpose of the school. Educators examine practices against—and reach consensus on the guarantees they will provide to every student based on—these foundational blocks. They are simultaneously a source of celebration and reflection, keeping collaborative teacher teams in PLCs grounded and providing the *legs* for the journey.

What Tim has done differently than most leaders of learning communities, however, is create a way to connect *students* to the mission, vision, values, and goals of his school community. His theme—building a brighter tomorrow, one brick at a time—takes the abstract concepts and ideas often expressed in mission, vision, values, and goals statements and makes them approachable for elementary students. He then worked to reinforce those ideas through challenge assemblies and gave students tangible ways they could participate in efforts to strengthen their school community. The result was that students at Campbell Elementary saw themselves as essential contributors to an important, shared effort. No longer was school a place where adults make all the important decisions or complete all the important work. Regardless of their age, Campbell Elementary students knew just what *they* could do to move their building forward.

Tim intentionally integrated elements of Wilbur Brookover and Lawrence Lezotte's (1979) effective schools research into the work of Campbell Elementary. Brookover and Lezotte (1979) argue that highly effective schools have a "climate of high expectations" (p. 4) where students make learning a priority because goals and expectations are clearly communicated by every adult up and down the hallway. A notable finding in their research is that staff in struggling schools have "low opinions of their students' abilities" while conversely, staff in improving schools have "high opinions of student abilities" (Brookover & Lezotte, 1979, p. 5). The impact that a climate of high expectations can have on the achievement of learners has been echoed by researchers and school change experts again and again, confirming Brookover and Lezotte's findings (DuFour et al., 2016; Fuchs, Fuchs, Mathes, Lipsey, & Roberts, 2002; Hattie, 2009; Jackson, 2011, Williams & Hierck, 2015).

Learning-centered schools do not just *communicate* messages about the ability of every student to achieve, however. Instead, learning-centered schools define *specific actions* that everyone can take to turn those core beliefs into reality. By articulating his vision in approachable language and then defining practical steps that students could take to move toward that vision, Tim brought the first big idea of the PLC at Work process—"a focus on learning"—to life for learners (DuFour et al., 2016). The success of his students happened not just because of the programs and structures that Campbell Elementary had in place to support learning. Rather, his students were successful because every member of the Campbell community— staff, students, and parents—believed that nothing could keep them from reaching their shared goals. They spoke about this belief together, sang about this belief together, and regularly celebrated progress made toward achieving this goal together.

Stated another way, Tim was intentionally using well-established rituals, symbols, and traditions to shape the *culture* of his school—a strategy widely recognized in the literature on organizational leadership (Bolman & Deal, 2011; Groysberg, Lee, Price, & Cheng, 2018; Jeffrey, 2018; Taylor, 2017). Rituals and traditions, when authentic, "touch the heart" (Bolman & Deal, 2011, p. 137) of—and tie together—community members. Rituals and traditions also build significance into the regular work of employees, preventing organizations from becoming "empty and sterile" (Bolman & Deal, 2011, p. 137) spaces. As simple as Tim's challenge assemblies may seem on the surface, those yellow hard hats, construction paper bricks, and customized theme song helped to communicate a cultural norm of high expectations to the Campbell Elementary school community, and a cultural norm well-communicated and repeatedly reinforced eventually becomes a defining and enduring characteristic of an organization (Groysberg et al., 2018). More importantly, a cultural norm well-communicated and repeatedly reinforced "can unleash tremendous amounts of energy toward a shared purpose and foster an organization's capacity to thrive" (Groysberg et al., 2018).

What Can This Look Like in Your Classroom?

Tim was first introduced to the importance of rituals and traditions as tools for communicating culture and adding significance to daily routines by Richard DuFour, long-time high school principal and one of the architects—along with Robert Eaker—of the PLC at Work process. Rick DuFour set the tone at Adlai Stevenson High School in Lincolnshire, Illinois, on his first day as building principal by calling the entire student body to an assembly in the gymnasium. Sitting by grade levels, the 1,800 students gathered for what would be a different beginning of the school year.

Rick welcomed the students to the school and introduced himself. He shared his enthusiasm and talked about his beliefs. He described the mission of the school and the commitment of the staff to helping every student succeed. He boldly predicted that within a few years, Adlai Stevenson High School would be recognized as one of the most outstanding public high schools in America by earning National Blue Ribbon status. He told the students that he had met with the teachers and felt strongly that their commitment, *along with the commitment of the students*, would take this school to new heights (Kanold, 2021; T. Kanold, personal communication, February 15, 2021).

He then asked the students to join with him in this effort. He called on all the freshmen to stand and follow his lead. "Sing with me!" he announced, before breaking into his own version of the refrain from the legendary Ike and Tina Turner cover of Sly and the Family Stone's, "I Want to Take You Higher" He turned to each class and asked them to do the same. "Sophomores! Juniors! Seniors!" By the time the seniors had joined in, "I Want to Take You Higher" had become a class rallying cry. Rick recognized the need to rally the students to become partners in accomplishing the BHAG of becoming a National Blue Ribbon School. Since Rick's tenure, Adlai Stevenson has gone on to become one of the most recognized public high schools in the United States, and they have received the National Blue Ribbon Award four times (Illinois Report Card, 2020; U.S. News and World Report, 2021).

What can you do to rally your students to become partners in accomplishing BHAGs? You can (1) create a chant, motto, or slogan; (2) develop classroom commitments or norms with students; (3) generate student promise statements; and (4) fill success walls with evidence of learning. We explore these strategies in the following sections.

Create a Chant, Motto, or Slogan

Daniel Goleman (2005), author of *Emotional Intelligence: Why It Can Matter More Than IQ*, argues that one of the best ways to strengthen teams in the corporate world is to engage groups of diverse individuals in "sustained camaraderie and daily efforts towards a common goal" (p. 159). Working together toward a common goal can "inspire significant effort and collaboration" and can leave individual members of teams with "the satisfaction of doing something worthy and meaningful" (Campbell & Sandino, 2019, p. 1). Like any educator well-versed in PLC at Work concepts, principals Tim Brown and Rick DuFour both knew just how critically important a clearly stated and simple vision is to creating a shared goal for a school. A clearly stated, simple vision provides direction for every decision in a PLC. More important, such a vision ensures consistency in both action and deed. It is easy for the members of a faculty with a clearly stated, simple vision to work together because they know exactly what it is that they are trying to create with one another.

But Tim and Rick also knew just how critically important it was to connect *students* to the school's vision, too. Doing so resulted in higher levels of investment and motivation from their building's most important stakeholders—the students. Those higher levels of investment and motivation allowed both Campbell Elementary and Adlai Stevenson High School to meet many of their BHAGs.

How did Tim and Rick connect students to the vision of their school? They started by developing simple slogans that communicated important expectations to their students. Campbell Elementary Cougars knew they were a part of building a better tomorrow together, and they could each contribute "one brick at a time" to those efforts by giving their best no matter how challenging their classwork seemed and by showing empathy to their peers. Patriots at Stevenson High School knew from day one that by holding one another to high expectations and by matching the commitment to excellence of classroom teachers and building leaders, they were going to "take each other higher."

There is nothing surprising here, right? Many schools have chants, mottos, or slogans that have become a part of the culture of the school. Here are just a few that we have run across.

- "With the courage to explore, the adventure begins."
- "In an Olympic year, go for the gold."
- "Dig deeper to find hidden treasures."
- "Shoot for the top, never the bottom, and not the middle."
- "It's time to show what we know."
- "We are a world-class school."
- "Opportunity starts with ME."
- "Make it a great day or not; the choice is yours."
- "Effort drives excellence."

The difference at Campbell Elementary and Adlai Stevenson, however, is that their slogans were used as *constant reminders* of the mission, vision, values, and goals of the school. Students knew they were a part of something bigger because they heard their teachers and principals emphasizing that larger purpose repeatedly. These slogans were not just printed on t-shirts and hung on banners at the school entrance, only to be forgotten. They were modeled and celebrated in classroom after classroom and assembly after assembly, building a genuine sense of unity and excitement in students.

If you are a secondary teacher interested in turning your school's chant, motto, or slogan into something more meaningful than it currently is, start by examining your school's chant, motto, or slogan. Use a process such as the one in figure 1.1 (page 12) to begin a conversation with students about just what your chant, motto, or slogan really means. When your students are finished reflecting, ask them to think about ways—short videos, informational posters, moments of reflection built into student activities— to raise awareness about the meaning of your school's chant, motto, or slogan.

If you are a primary teacher, streamline this process by concentrating your classroom conversation on the four questions that appear in step 2 of figure 1.1.

1. If students were honoring our school's chant, motto, or slogan, what would we see them doing?

2. If teachers were honoring our school's chant, motto, or slogan, what would we see them doing?

3. If parents were honoring our school's chant, motto, or slogan, what would we see them doing?

4. If principals were honoring our school's chant, motto, or slogan, what would we see them doing?

Whether you are a primary or secondary teacher, leading your students through a conversation about the meaning behind your school's chant, motto, or slogan will send the message that your building's mission, vision, values, and goals are more than a collection of words hanging on banners around your hallway. Instead, they are a promise that members of your school community are making to one another each day that they come to school.

Step 1: Work in a small group of three or four students to answer the following questions.						
What is our school's chant, motto, or slogan?						
How often do you hear our school's chant, motto, or slogan? (Circle a number on the rating scale that best represents your answer to this question.)						
Never	1	2	3	4	5	In every class, every day
How often do you think about our school's chant, motto, or slogan? (Circle a number on the rating scale that best represents your answer to this question.)						
Never	1	2	3	4	5	All the time
How well do you understand the meaning behind our school's chant, motto, or slogan? (Circle a number on the rating scale that best represents your answer to this question.)						
I did not know it had a meaning.	1	2	3	4	5	I could easily explain the meaning to others.

Reflection Questions

Chants, mottos, and slogans are often used in both sports and in advertising. Find an example of a chant, motto, or slogan that is an effective tool for building unity with or communicating expectations to fans or customers. What makes it effective?

Do you think our school's chant, motto, or slogan is an effective tool for building unity with or communicating expectations to students? Why?

What could our school do to make our chant, motto, or slogan a more effective tool for building unity with or communicating expectations to both students and teachers?

Step 2: Work in a small group of three or four students to answer the following questions.

If **students** were honoring our school's chant, motto, or slogan, what would we see them DOING?	If **teachers** were honoring our school's chant, motto, or slogan, what would we see them DOING?
If **parents** were honoring our school's chant, motto, or slogan, what would we see them DOING?	If **principals** were honoring our school's chant, motto, or slogan, what would we see them DOING?

Now, design a plan for building knowledge about the meaning of our school's chant, motto, or slogan.

Be ready to share your answers with your classmates! Choose a spokesperson to summarize your group's thinking.

Figure 1.1: Tool for examining a school's chant, motto, or slogan.

Secondary teachers interested in leading students through a conversation about the meaning behind their school's chant, motto, or slogan can find a blank template titled "Looking Closely at What Our School's Chant, Motto, or Slogan Means" on page 21. Primary teachers who like Tim's "Building a Brighter Tomorrow" idea spotlighted at the beginning of this chapter can find a brick template in figure 1.2 (see also the reproducible "Earning a Brick to Add to Our School's Foundation" on page 23 to use with students).

By working with students to develop an explicit set of action steps that everyone can take to ensure that they have a great school year together, teachers make it possible for the students in their classrooms to exert daily efforts toward a common goal. The result will be a team of students who can achieve more together than they would have ever accomplished on their own.

Develop Classroom Commitments or Norms With Students

In the PLC at Work process, collaborative teams of teachers spend significant time developing norms, agreements on how they will behave to work effectively together. In fact, norms, values, and collective commitments are considered foundational elements of a PLC (DuFour et al., 2016). They are not *handed to groups*, but instead, they are *developed by groups*. Norms, values, and collective commitments allow the members of a collaborative team to bring their voices to the table to communicate what they need from others for their learning to be enhanced.

Hal Urban, a former high school social studies teacher at San Carlos and Woodside High Schools, used a similar process with his students (H. Urban, personal communication, October 17, 2005). Early in every school year, Hal and the colleagues on his collaborative team engaged their students in an opportunity to develop a set of collective commitments with one another. They started by explaining to students that the world we live in requires a greater understanding of—and appreciation for—people than ever before. Then, they asked students to think about the commitments that they would have to make if they were truly going to learn *with* and *from* each other over the course of the school year. Students worked in groups of four to answer the following questions together.

1. If we are to have high levels of learning, what should the relationship between student and teacher be like in this classroom?

2. If we are to learn from each other, what should the relationship between student and student be like in this classroom?

_____
(Student Name)

HAS HELPED OUR SCHOOL TO BUILD A BRIGHTER TOMORROW TOGETHER BY:

Figure 1.2: Brick for building a brighter tomorrow activity.

3. Sometimes learning means struggling through something to find the answer. When you struggle, how can the teacher help you?

4. What have you found to be helpful in the past when you are having difficulty mastering a concept?

Once groups were finished processing, Hal led a classroom discussion, having each group report their thinking. While groups were reporting, he charted the patterns in student responses on the classroom whiteboard. Together, Hal's class turned those patterns into pledges that defined how they would interact with one another over the course of the upcoming school year. What is worth noting in the work that Hal did with his students to develop a set of classroom commitments? Creating a culture of learning in a classroom is never an accident. Rather, it requires that teachers and students spend time deliberately discussing the expectations that they have for one another.

Another popular variation of Hal's strategy is to have students start the school year by responding to the following four prompts on sticky notes.

1. "To make this class great, I will . . ."

2. "I want students in our class to . . ."

3. "In order to succeed in this class, I will . . ."

4. "My teacher can help me succeed by . . ."

Once students have finished responding, sort their sticky notes by prompt into four quadrants on your classroom whiteboard. Then, ask a group of student leaders to review the patterns in the actions that members of your class believe are essential for succeeding with one another. After they have grouped comments addressing similar behaviors, have your student leaders create a short list of action steps for each of the four questions in the prompts. Finally, turn those lists of action steps into a table that students can keep in the front of their notebooks as a constant reminder of the specific behaviors that both teachers and students can take to help your class meet their shared goals together (figure 1.3).

While teachers working in grades preK–2 may not have students responding to these prompts on sticky notes and sorting those stickies into quadrants to look for patterns, we would argue that a classroom conversation held early in the school year about the same four prompts is just as important for the youngest learners as it is for students in grades 3–12. Remember, norms are the common patterns of participation in any group, whether that group consists of adults or primary students. Also remember that every group has norms, whether you talk openly about them or not. Helping students to understand that some patterns of participation make it easier for us to learn together and other patterns of participation can get in the way of learning is an important lesson for learners of any age.

Educators interested in integrating classroom norms and collective commitments into their work with students can use the reproducibles, "Developing Classroom Norms" and "Self-Reflecting on Our Classroom Norms," on pages 24 and 26.

Our Vision of What We Can Do to Have a Great School Year Together	
To make this class great, I will . . . • Try to cooperate with everyone • Offer lots of good suggestions and ask a lot of good questions • Do my best to be in a good mood every day	**I want students in our class to . . .** • Think of everyone as a friend • Be willing to lend a hand when classmates are struggling • Do their part on any group tasks that we have
To succeed in this class, I will . . . • Come to class prepared and ready to learn • Complete every assignment that I am asked to complete • Work hard instead of work fast	**My teacher can help me succeed by . . .** • Understanding that we all learn in different ways • Being patient when we aren't having our best days • Giving us second (and third) chances when we need them

Figure 1.3: Our vision of what we can do to have a great school year together.

While teachers can easily adopt either of the strategies from these reproducibles, remember that *it is not the strategy that matters most*. Instead, what matters most is setting aside time to engage students in conversations about the kinds of behaviors that can move a group forward together. Those conversations give teachers the opportunity to highlight the idea of learning, of mastering content, and of working together. Those conversations also give teachers the chance to communicate a sense of hope, determination, confidence, and drive to their students. Finally, those conversations help build positive interpersonal relationships, to show intensity and enthusiasm, and to create a welcoming classroom environment.

Also remember that for commitments and norms to become meaningful, educators must find ways to regularly reinforce them. Start by pointing out moments in classroom interactions when you notice individual students or small groups who are honoring the norms. Simple statements like, "I just saw Tyreek and Makayla being patient with one another" or "I'm proud of Luke, who asked a ton of good questions in class today" go a long way toward reminding students of the patterns of participation that are necessary for ensuring that your class is successful together. You can also set aside time at the end of lessons to give students the opportunity to recognize peers who have honored your classroom commitments. Finally, you can ask your students to review your classroom's norms or collective commitments periodically, identifying personal strengths and areas for improvement.

Generate Student Promise Statements

Using chants, mottos, and slogans, or sets of norms and collective commitments with students is a great first step toward reinforcing a culture of learning in your school or classroom. Doing so results in a set of shared expectations that everyone—parents, students, teachers, principals—can measure themselves against. More important, chants, mottos, slogans, norms, and collective commitments can be used to set a shared direction for your school community. When everyone agrees to build a better future together *and* has a sense for just what building a better future looks like in action, they can make individual contributions to the work of the whole.

For many students, however, making individual contributions to the work of the whole can be an abstract concept. When progressing through childhood and adolescence, students are naturally egocentric, believing that others see, hear, and think in the same ways that they do (McLeod, 2018). In addition, we live in an increasingly isolated world where working with neighbors to create something better together is no longer the norm. In fact, as membership in mission-driven community organizations that once held us together—4-H clubs, Scout troops, church youth groups, Rotary clubs, Lions Clubs—dwindles (Crary, 2018; Heinonen, 2019; Newby & Sallee, 2011; Schmidt & Epstein, 2019), it is far more likely for students to live across the street from neighbors whom they have never met than it is for students to take part in shared efforts to advance the common good with their neighbors.

How can teachers reinforce the notion that advancing the common good depends on the actions and decisions of individual members of a community? They can ask their students to develop *promise statements* that are connected to the broader mission, vision, values, and goals of the classroom or school community. Developing student promise statements starts by asking students to respond to simple prompts like, "Looking back at our classroom norms, what are some steps that you are willing to take to make our year together safe, happy, and successful?" or "What kinds of things can you do as an individual to live up to the ideas expressed in our school's slogan?" The goal is to encourage students to think about who they currently are, who they most want to become, and how they can best contribute to the shared work of the class. Then, teachers can ask students to generate one- or two-sentence statements that express the promise that they are willing to make to their peers.

Here are a few examples of student promise statements.

- "I will learn new things each day so that I am ready for the real world."
- "I will enjoy school, respect my classmates, and be a leader every day!"
- "I will study, learn, and make friends by listening to others in order to gain knowledge."
- "I will help my classmates by lending a hand when they are struggling with schoolwork

and be patient with them when they are having a bad day."

- "I will make contributions to the learning of our class by asking lots of questions when I am confused or when I have made a neat discovery."

- "I will help our classroom to be safe, happy, and successful by always showing respect to my classmates—even when I disagree with them."

Like the chants, mottos, and slogans we introduced earlier in this chapter, the development of student promise statements must be something more than a one-time event. If student promise statements are going to strengthen the shared commitments of your classroom, students need to have regular opportunities to reflect on whether they are living up to the promises that they have made to their peers. To encourage this reflection, start by having students record their promise statements in the front of their notebooks. Then, have students design small posters sharing their individual statements to hang on a *promise wall* in your classroom. Finally, throughout the school year, ask students to stop and reflect on their promise statements. Start these moments of reflection by asking, "What are some things that you need to start doing—or stop doing—in order to better honor your promises to our classroom?"

Use the reproducible tools "Developing Student Promise Statements" and "Self-Reflecting on My Promise Statement" on pages 27 and 28 to integrate student promise statements into the regular work of your classroom.

Fill Classroom Walls With Evidence of Learning

In *The Data Coach's Guide to Improving Learning for All Students: Unleashing the Power of Collaborative Inquiry*, Nancy B. Love, Katherine E. Stiles, Susan E. Mundry, and Kathryn DiRanna (2008) suggest that collaborative teams working with assessment results should turn data sets into large charts to display on data walls for all to see. "Go visual with your data," they argue, "to help construct meaning, make sense, and prepare to engage in meaningful dialogue" (p. 7). We argue that "going visual" with data is also a great strategy for reinforcing a culture of learning for students. One simple way to go visual with data in your classroom is to post simple achievement charts displaying the classroom average on both pretests and post-tests (figure 1.4).

As you post new achievement charts, take a few moments in class to point out the changes from pretest to post-test. Explain to your students that this difference is not an accident. Ask students probing questions such as the following.

- "What is working for us as a class?"

- "How are your participation and collaboration impacting your peers and our results?"

PROOF THAT WE ARE LEARNERS

Our class average on our place value pretest:

41

Our class average on our week-two place value quiz:

79

Figure 1.4: Sample classroom achievement chart.

- "What learning strategies should we continue using?"
- "Are there any learning strategies that we should abandon?"

These conversations help students see that growth over time is a product of their own actions and the actions of the entire class. That message is fundamentally empowering, helping students to realize that they really *can* have a positive impact on learning outcomes.

Another strategy to try is to create achievement charts showing a frequency distribution of grades earned on both pretests and post-tests. See the example in figure 1.5.

Notice that this classroom achievement chart starts with a clear statement of a classroom goal: By the end of our unit on place value, all students will score an 80 percent or above on our final exam. Stating a classroom goal provides all students with motivation to work toward mastery. More important, stating a classroom goal provides all students *with motivation to help their classmates* to work toward mastery as well. Also, notice that individual scores students earn on both the pretest and the post-test are recorded with a simple dot. Hanging side-by-side, it is easy to see that those dots—which represent the learning of the class—move

forward from lower to higher levels of mastery from the pretest to the post-test. That pattern tells an important story to students. That is, *our classroom's business is learning*. We know more after we are done with our lessons and our practice than we did when we started. And everyone is making contributions to our classroom because every dot has moved forward. We may not be perfect at the end of instruction—not everyone has met our classroom goal of earning an 80 percent on our post-test yet. But we do know that we can make progress because we are all learners.

If you decide to work with achievement charts that include frequency distributions, it is important to keep individual student scores anonymous. The best way to do that is to ask your students to think about the patterns that they can spot on classroom achievement charts a day or two before you hand back graded assignments to students. Doing so will keep students focused on spotting general trends in the progress the class makes instead of trying to compare their own performance to the performance of their peers. Remember, you are trying to protect the intellectual reputation of your students and to build your class's confidence in their ability to move forward. That can only be done when students are freed from the pressure that comes along with looking at the scores their

Our Goal: All students will score an 80 percent or above on the post-test for our upcoming unit on place value.

Scores Earned	Our Pretest Results	Our Post-Test Results
100	● ●	● ● ● ●
90	●	● ● ● / ● ● ●
80	● ● ●	● ● ● ● ● / ● ● ● ● ●
70	● ● ●	● ● ●
60	● ● ● ● ● ● / ● ● ● ●	●
50 or less	● ● ● / ● ● ●	

Figure 1.5: Sample classroom achievement chart with frequency distribution.

classmates earn on graded assignments. Anonymity makes that possible.

Can you see how powerful classroom success walls can be? Tim and Rick used chants and slogans as constant reminders of the mission and purpose of the school. You can also use *evidence of learning* to accomplish that same goal. Each mastery conversation you have after posting a new achievement chart to your classroom success wall becomes a tangible reminder to students that it is their responsibility to learn, and each set of before and after data provides proof that students really do have what it takes to meet the high expectations you have for them.

Whether you decide to create mottos, write norms, generate promise statements, or develop a classroom success wall, remember that your main goal is to find ways to rally your students as partners in accomplishing the BHAGs set by your school community. Recognize your students as essential stakeholders in the success of the community and work to find, choose, develop, modify, and tailor instructional strategies that connect students to the mission, vision, values, and goals of your school in an age-appropriate way. Doing so takes ideas that are typically reserved for the adults in a PLC at Work and turns them into powerful tools to motivate, inspire, and challenge students.

Recommendations for Getting Started

If it is true that culture begins with agreed-on mission, vision, values, and goals, then educators must do all that we can to make sure that the mission, vision, values, and goals of our building become something more than just words on a website or a banner. Instead, our mission, vision, values, and goals must be evident in what teachers and other educators and staff members say and do in every classroom, every day. The following section outlines our most important recommendations for ensuring that your school's mission, vision, values, and goals are consistently communicated to students.

Start From Day One

There are certain routines that are almost universally followed on the first day of class in most secondary schools: teachers pass out the course syllabus, go over rules and procedures, assign books or devices to

students, do an ice-breaker activity, and start teaching. But another routine happens on the first day of school, too. Students leave their classrooms at the end of the day and come back to their homes and neighborhoods where they are almost immediately asked, "How was your first day?" by their peers, parents, guardians, and siblings.

This question makes the first day of school so much more important than we might have imagined. Everything that educators do and say in those first moments in the classroom with students sets the tone for the entire year; once they are gone, we cannot get those moments back. Whether we like it or not, all students head home at the end of the day excited, neutral, or dreading the fact that they have been assigned to a particular class.

What does that mean for teachers interested in building a commitment to learning in students? It means that we need to rethink our first-day routines. If we want to use our first moments with students to set high expectations for learning, we need to do something more than go over the syllabus and start teaching. Instead, the tasks that we choose—like those connected to the tools and strategies spotlighted in the previous section of this chapter—need to be intentionally designed to tap into the sense of hope and anticipation that every learner feels on the first day of school. Students need to leave their classrooms knowing that they are a part of something bigger than themselves and convinced that they can take steps to move both themselves and the entire school community forward. Stated another way, we need to send the message from day one that this year is going to be different—and that *different is better*.

Start From Grade One

We have seen in our work in schools across the globe that many practitioners question whether primary students—kids in kindergarten, first, and second grade—can handle conversations about the role they can play in advancing the mission, vision, values, and goals of their school community. "Those concepts are too abstract for our young students," they argue. "That's work best left for teachers in the upper grades."

That argument sells both primary teachers and their students short. The strongest practitioners know that important concepts can be introduced in any grade level if teachers use their expertise to develop age-appropriate lessons or to structure age-appropriate conversations. Sure, primary students will struggle with terms like "shared mission, vision, values, and goals"—but repackaging those concepts as "working together to accomplish something important" or "keeping our promises to one another" is a simple step that practitioners can take to connect even the youngest students to the big, hairy, audacious goals that stand at the center of a school's purpose.

In fact, starting conversations about your school's mission, vision, values, and goals in your primary classrooms might just be the *most important* step you can take if you really want a commitment to learning to become a part of the culture of your school. Here is why: Older students already have a sense of school values and beliefs based on years of interactions with teachers and students in your building. Changing those assumptions will take more than just a new motto or set of norms. Instead, it is going to take both time and lots of firsthand experience. Primary students, however, are just being introduced to the culture in your school building. That means students in primary classrooms will more readily learn new lessons about who we are and what we believe, and as those students move forward, they will carry those lessons learned from one grade level to the next.

Make It Universal

Anyone could grab a strategy highlighted in this chapter and start implementing it tomorrow. They are all well-designed, easy to pull together and deliver, and—with some simple modification—can be used at any grade level. Whether they choose to create a new slogan, write classroom norms, generate student promise statements, or develop classroom success walls, teachers who embrace these strategies could successfully build a commitment to learning *in their individual classrooms.*

But if you are a school leader—a teacher working on a school-improvement team, a principal with a passion for improving your building, a coach who supports teams at multiple grade levels—you already know that to change the culture of an entire school, we need to think beyond the actions individual teachers take to reimagine the work being done inside their classrooms. Culture is the *shared* values, beliefs, and

behaviors of an organization (Muhammad, 2017; Watkins, 2013)—not the values, beliefs, and behaviors of a small group of individuals within the organization. To change the culture of an entire school, then, schools will need to identify strategies to implement systematically across grade levels. Doing so will ensure that students—regardless of the grade level they are in or the teacher they are assigned to—will be exposed repeatedly to the same set of core beliefs and attitudes toward learning.

Identifying those shared strategies is work that should start in a PLC's school leadership team. Representatives from all grade levels and departments can discuss the beliefs and behaviors most important to communicate to students and then modify shared instructional practices, designing lessons that are simultaneously consistent and age-appropriate for students across grade levels. Once a leadership team has settled on a small handful of strategies worth trying, members can communicate those strategies to their collaborative teams and offer support as their peers begin to implement new practices in their classrooms.

Take It Slow

We offer another piece of advice for school leaders that is a *don't.* Don't ask teachers to try to tackle every strategy introduced in this chapter all at the same time. Like any new practice introduced in schools, connecting students to your school's mission, vision, values, and goals comes with a learning curve for everyone. Teachers must first have a shared understanding of exactly what the school's mission, vision, values, and goals mean before they can change anything about the work they are doing in their classrooms. And students are going to have to begin to see themselves as valuable contributors to the mission of your school before they can change anything about the way that they interact with lessons, with their teachers, or with their peers. Both of those changes can be big asks for teachers and students already wrestling with the day-to-day demands of teaching and learning the required curriculum.

Instead, keep initial attempts at building a commitment to learning in students simple. Already have a school motto that is well known? Start there. Ask teachers to structure explicit conversations about what that motto means and why that motto matters.

Already have several teachers who are using the first days of school to develop shared sets of classroom procedures and rules with their students? Start there. Instead of focusing on simple procedural expectations during those conversations, teachers can emphasize behaviors connected to the school's mission, vision, values, and goals. Asking students, "How can we make our school year safe, happy, and successful?" is just as easy as asking, "What steps should a student in our classroom take if they are absent from school?" If teachers are already requiring students to keep data notebooks to track their progress toward mastering important outcomes, then start there. Turning data collected by individual students into a classroom success wall can be a useful addition to an existing practice that your teachers already believe in.

The key is to find logical and approachable next steps worth taking if connecting students to your mission, vision, values, and goals will be an important part of the way you do business in your school. The most successful change efforts are sustainable—and sustainable change depends on keeping things simple until leaders have built the capacity of both students and staff.

Concluding Thoughts

Identifying the school's mission, vision, values, and goals is an essential behavior for any PLC. Meaningful collaboration depends on ensuring that all staff members have a unified sense of purpose and that sense of purpose is articulated in the mission, vision, values, and goals statements. Prominently displayed proclamations crafted with great sincerity by the adults in a school community should be thought of as tools to motivate, inspire, rally, honor, drive, ignite, and light anew the efforts of the adults charged with working together to ensure success for all students. More important, prominently displayed proclamations crafted with great sincerity should be thought of as tools *to guide the actions of* the adults in the school. As

Learning by Doing authors DuFour, DuFour, Eaker, Many, and Mattos (2016) explain, "The words of a mission statement are not worth the paper that they are printed on unless people begin to *do* differently" (p. 34, emphasis in original).

It is just as vital that students share that unified sense of purpose. They are, after all, the most important stakeholders in a school community. If the primary goal of schools is to ensure high levels of *learning*, then educators need to see the mission, vision, values, and goals as tools for motivating, inspiring, and guiding the actions of *learners*. In fact, we would argue that the major difference between highly functioning learning communities and those that struggle to produce results is not that *the staff* have a shared sense of purpose. Instead, it is that the staff have deliberately crafted plans for—and followed through on—communicating these foundational concepts to *their students*. Stated another way, a commitment to high levels of learning in a school does not start when the adults agree to it. A commitment to high levels of learning in a school starts when the students believe in it.

For some teachers—particularly those in buildings without a strong, unifying sense of purpose—deliberately crafting plans for communicating foundational concepts to students is going to feel like just another thing to do. And there is no doubt that taking this step will require time for discussion, dialogue, and debate as the adults consider the key messages and actions that each teacher and administrator would advance to their students. These conversations may even make some staff members uncomfortable. It might be—after all—the first time they have ever been challenged to connect their instructional practices to the descriptions of the school the community wants to become and the goals they want to achieve.

The result, however, will be a sharing of ideals, messages, and actions that can reinforce the school's mission, vision, values, and goals in the hearts and minds of every stakeholder, including students.

Looking Closely at What Our School's Chant, Motto, or Slogan Means

Chants, mottos, and slogans are designed to build a sense of unity and commitment in students and teachers. They are also designed to communicate shared expectations to students and teachers in an easy-to-understand way. Today, we are going to look closely at what our school's chant, motto, or slogan means.

Step 1: Work in a small group of three or four students to answer the following questions.

What is our school's chant, motto, or slogan?						
How often do you hear our school's chant, motto, or slogan? *(Circle a number on the rating scale that best represents your answer to this question.)*						
Never	1	2	3	4	5	In every class, every day
How often do you think about our school's chant, motto, or slogan? *(Circle a number on the rating scale that best represents your answer to this question.)*						
Never	1	2	3	4	5	All the time
How well do you understand the meaning behind our school's chant, motto, or slogan? *(Circle a number on the rating scale that best represents your answer to this question.)*						
I did not know it had a meaning.	1	2	3	4	5	I could easily explain the meaning to others.
Reflection Questions						

1. Chants, mottos, and slogans are often used in both sports and in advertising. Find an example of a chant, motto, or slogan that is an effective tool for building unity with or communicating expectations to fans or customers. What makes it effective?

2. Do you think our school's chant, motto, or slogan is an effective tool for building unity with or communicating expectations to students? Why?

page 1 of 2

3. What could our school do to make our chant, motto, or slogan a more effective tool for building unity with or communicating expectations to both students and teachers?

Step 2: Work in a small group of three or four students to answer the following questions.

If **students** were honoring our school's chant, motto, or slogan, what would we see them DOING?	If **teachers** were honoring our school's chant, motto, or slogan, what would we see them DOING?
If **parents** were honoring our school's chant, motto, or slogan, what would we see them DOING?	If **principals** were honoring our school's chant, motto, or slogan, what would we see them DOING?

Now, design a plan for building knowledge about the meaning of our school's chant, motto, or slogan.

Be ready to share your answers with your classmates!
Choose a spokesperson to summarize your group's thinking.

page 2 of 2

Earning a Brick to Add to Our School's Foundation

As you know, our school's motto this year is, "Let's Build a Brighter Tomorrow Together, One Brick at a Time." Even as a student, you can help us to build that future by following through on our classroom's promises to one another. Each time you follow through on one of those promises, you will get to fill out a construction paper brick that will be added to the display in the main hallway of our school at the end of each of our weekly challenge assemblies.

How many bricks will YOU earn this year?

There are LOTS of ways that you can earn a brick for honoring our classroom's promises to one another. Here are a few examples.

Earning a terrific mark on a difficult assignment	Reworking a task that you struggled to complete the first time around	Lending a hand to a friend who missed class and is trying to get caught up
Cleaning up your workspace consistently	Asking a question in class that makes everyone think	Using a respectful tone when speaking with students you disagree with
Helping a peer understand a concept that you have already mastered	Listening carefully during classroom conversations	Showing up to class on time and ready to work

When your teacher awards you a brick, your job is to cut it out and bring it to the next challenge assembly.

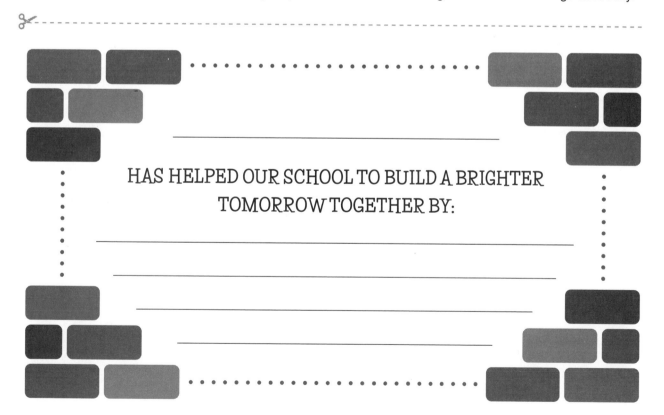

HAS HELPED OUR SCHOOL TO BUILD A BRIGHTER TOMORROW TOGETHER BY:

Developing Classroom Norms

To make sure that we have a great year together in our classroom, we are going to write some classroom norms. Norms are simple statements that describe the actions that we all agree to follow. We will follow the steps on this handout to build our classroom norms.

Step 1: Brainstorm on Your Own

Working by yourself, please brainstorm two or three endings for each of the sentence starters below.

To make this class great, I will . . .	I want students in our class to . . .
To succeed in this class, I will . . .	My teacher can help me to succeed by . . .

Now copy the MOST IMPORTANT action step from each box onto a sticky note.

Then, place it in the right quadrant on our classroom's dry-erase board. Members of our class will sort and summarize our statements to create a list of three actions for each box that we will review and vote on.

Step 2: Review Your Classroom's Norms

Working with a partner, review the norms that your classmates chose as a summary of the actions that we would take if we were going to have a great year together in our classroom. While reviewing the norms that they have chosen, think about the following four questions.

Question	Your Response
Which norm on the draft that our classmates produced is the most important for people to honor? What makes this norm so important?	

page 1 of 2

Question	Your Response
Which norm do you think will be the hardest for members of our class to follow? What makes this norm so difficult to honor?	
Are there any norms that you just cannot agree to follow? Why?	
Have any important norms been left off the draft that our classmates produced? Which ones?	

Step 3: Make Your Voice Heard

Now, it is time to express how you feel about our classroom norms. Shade the statement below that best represents your feelings about our norms. Then, write a few sentences that explain the reason for your feelings.

I like these norms just like they are.	For the most part, I like these norms, but I think we should make a few revisions.	There is no way that I can agree to follow these norms.
My Reasoning:		

Self-Reflecting on Our Classroom Norms

Earlier during the school year, we worked together to create a set of classroom norms. Those norms are promises that we made to each other to ensure that we have a great school year together. Answer the questions below to reflect on how well you are honoring our classroom norms.

Step 1: Give Yourself an Overall Rating

Shade the number in the rating bar below that best represents your work toward honoring our classroom norms.

I **NEVER** honor our classroom norms.	1	2	3	4	5	I **ALWAYS** honor our classroom norms.

Step 2: Reflection Questions

Answer the questions below to think more about the work that you are doing to honor our classroom norms.

Question	Your Response
Which classroom norm do you do the best job honoring?	
Why is this norm easy for you to honor?	
Which classroom norm do you struggle to honor?	
What makes it difficult for you to honor this norm?	
Who does a great job honoring the norm that you struggle with?	
How is his or her behavior or his or her choices different from yours in this area?	
What changes are you going to make in the next few weeks to improve your efforts to honor our classroom norms?	

Developing Student Promise Statements

If we are going to have a safe, happy, and successful school year, we are all going to have to promise to take actions that will improve the work that we do with one another.

Here are some examples of actions to take:

I will learn new things each day so that I am ready for the real world.	I will enjoy school, respect my classmates, and be a LEADER every day!	I will study, learn, and make friends by listening to others.
I will help my classmates by lending a hand when they are struggling with schoolwork and being patient with them when they are having a bad day.	I will make contributions to the learning of our class by asking lots of questions when I am confused or when I have made a neat discovery!	I will help our classroom to be safe, happy, and successful by always showing respect to my classmates, even when I disagree with them.

So what promise are you willing to make to help us to have a safe, happy, and successful school year?

Record your promise in the following box.

To help us have a safe, happy, and successful school year, I promise to:

Question	Your Response
How will your promise help to make our school year safe, happy, and successful? What impact will your promise have on your peers? Will it help them to learn more? Will it help them to look forward to school more? Will it help them to feel welcome in our classroom?	
Why is this the right promise for YOU to make to your peers? Is this promise something you already do well—or is it something that you are hoping to improve on over the course of the school year?	

Self-Reflecting on My Promise Statement

Over the course of the school year, we will stop several times to think about how well we are doing at honoring the promises that we made to our peers. We will record our reflections on this self-reflection template.

Rating Scale

I am **STRUGGLING** to honor my promise to my peers.	1	2	3	4	5	I am **SUCCEEDING** at honoring my promise to my peers.

Record of Self-Reflections

Date of Self-Reflection	Your Self-Rating	Can You Give an Example of a Time When You Honored Your Promise to Your Peers?	What Are Your Next Steps Going to Be?

2 Helping Students Understand the Expectations for a Unit of Study

Isabel, a hard-working third grader, received a social studies assignment to create a pamphlet about her state. Her teacher showed the class some examples from previous third graders, gave the students a list of websites to explore, and carved out time during class for the students to research. Even with exemplars to look at, Isabel was still somewhat unclear about the final product that she was supposed to produce, but she tackled the assignment with her usual dedication and desire to please. She went online to the websites her teacher shared, and, never having done research before, began to copy down information that she thought was important to know about her state.

As the due date for the assignment neared, Isabel was feeling anxious about the project. A few days before her work was to be turned in, she asked her mother for help. When her mother looked at the information Isabel had been copying from her computer searches, it was obvious that she was unclear about just what a good pamphlet should look like. Knowing that this was the first time that Isabel had ever researched a topic, Isabel's mother asked if the teacher had given the class a document explaining the expectations for the assignment. Isabel shared that the teacher had hung up some examples completed by students in previous years and told the students to write down things that they found interesting about their state, but that was it. There were some frustrating evenings at home as Isabel's mother began working with her to develop an organized pamphlet that Isabel could be proud of. She ended up receiving an A for her work on the assignment, but only because she asked her mother for help.

Can you see what is happening here? Like all educators working in a PLC, Isabel's teachers began their collaborative efforts by answering the first critical question of learning: What knowledge, skills, and dispositions should every student acquire as a result of this unit, this course, or this grade level? (DuFour et al., 2016). This question helps teams generate lists of concepts and behaviors that members can use to guide their collective inquiry with one another. While completing this work, Isabel's teachers also agreed on a task and product that they would use to assess student mastery of their identified essentials. That is, research your state and create a pamphlet for teaching others about what you have learned. Finally, Isabel's teachers worked together to build a list of websites that students could use to learn more about the state they live in.

But Isabel's teachers failed to align their expectations of what proficient levels of work would look like. Providing clarity and guidance for novice learners like Isabel requires the team to decide on the categorical and historical information students would be held accountable for including on their final pamphlets, and for articulating the research skills that a student would need to master to successfully meet their teachers' expectations. Providing clarity and guidance for novice learners like Isabel also requires the team to develop a plan for the following.

- Helping students set goals and plan action steps

- Helping students organize their work

- Providing students with specific, accurate, and timely feedback on their initial attempts at mastery

- Helping students track their own progress toward completing the assignment and meeting their teachers' expectations

- Communicating and clarifying expectations for the assignment to parents

Finally, providing clarity and guidance for novice learners like Isabel requires the team to clearly communicate their expectations to their *students*—a missing piece in the planning process for too many schools. "For many students," educational researcher John Hattie argues, "it is often not clear what teachers want them to do or understand, or what level of performance is required. Why should students be made to guess what the teacher means, wants and expects?" (as cited in Almarode & Vandas, 2019, Location No. 83).

That one pedagogical decision—establishing shared outcomes but failing to clearly communicate them to students—diminishes the meaning and relevance of those very same outcomes as tools for improving student learning. It is impossible to engage students as partners in the learning process when they are unsure of the success criterion for the tasks their teachers are asking them to tackle. On the other hand, students with a clear sense of the expectations for an assignment show higher levels of self-assessing, self-evaluating, self-monitoring, and self-learning than students who are forced to guess what you mean, want, and expect (Hattie, 2009, Location No. 1050).

That means developing high levels of self-efficacy in students depends on educators who work intentionally to communicate expectations to their students—a process we will explore in depth in the pages to come. We will begin by looking at research around the impact that sharing clear targets can have on student learning. Then, we will examine ways in which collaborative teams help students become more engaged with learning targets. Finally, we will share examples of processes, products, and protocols that teams have used to send the following important messages to their students.

1. There is a reason we want—and need—you to learn these concepts, skills, and behaviors.

2. We can show you what proficiency looks like, and we will be looking for it in your work.

3. What we are asking of you has been accomplished by other students in the past.

4. You can do this, and I am going to help you get there.

By the end of this chapter, you will have a better sense for the steps collaborative teams can take to turn their answers to the first critical question of learning into something more than just a list of essential outcomes *to focus the efforts of teachers*. We want to leave you convinced that when used correctly, lists of essential outcomes collaborative teams develop can become tools that also focus *the efforts of students*.

Why Is This Important to Learners?

One of the fundamental principles of learning that is both common sense *and* supported by evidence is the notion that students are more likely to hit a target when they know what the target is. That is why it has become standard procedure to post learning goals on the board at the front of the classroom each day. While this common practice has a premise rooted in research, too often it has become nothing more than an act of compliance for teachers hoping to meet one of the look fors of the classroom walkthrough process.

Look closely at the research, however, and you will find that clarifying learning outcomes for students matters more than you might realize. Take the work of Hattie (TEDx Talks, 2013), for example: When reporting on his findings of meta-analyses of decades of educational research, Hattie argues that outside of collaborating closely with colleagues, the single most important step that a teacher can take to improve achievement in their classrooms is to show "the students up front what success looks like when they are beginning a task." That step—which Hattie calls "the power of moving from what students know now towards explicit success criteria" (TEDx Talks, 2013)—has a greater impact on learning than class size initiatives, technology integration efforts, or students' home circumstances.

Hattie's belief in the importance of clarifying learning outcomes for students is echoed by Robert

Marzano (2007), who started his influential book on instruction—*The Art and Science of Teaching*—with a simple argument: Establishing and communicating learning goals is a foundational behavior of highly successful teachers. Marzano (2017) built on the importance of clarifying learning outcomes for students in *The New Art and Science of Teaching*, stating that, "If students understand what they are to learn during a given lesson or unit, they are better able to determine how well they are doing and what they need to improve" (p. 11). Marzano makes it clear in both texts, however, that clarifying essential outcomes alone is not enough to improve student learning. Instead, it is essential to track student progress using formative assessment, another research-supported strategy for both teachers and learners that we will explore in greater depth in chapter 3. For Marzano, establishing and communicating learning goals must always come first. "After all," he writes, "for learning to be effective, clear targets in terms of information and skill must be established" (Marzano, 2007, p. 9).

The impact of providing clarity on what students should know and be able to do is also a common principle in the work of Rick Stiggins and his colleagues at the Assessment Training Institute. Through his studies and writings on formative assessment, he has articulated the kinds of strategies that "assessment literate" teachers use to bring assessment into the learning process and turn assessments into tools to motivate students to strive for higher levels of learning (Chappuis, Commodore, & Stiggins, 2016, p. 76). Consider some of the strategies that follow and note how many depend on helping students become knowledgeable about the learning outcomes they are expected to achieve.

- Teachers understand and can articulate *in advance of teaching* the achievement targets students are to hit.

- *Students are informed regularly* about those targets in terms they can understand, in part through the study of the criteria by which their work will be evaluated and samples of high-quality work. As a result, *students can describe what targets they are to hit* and what comes next in their learning.

- Teachers involve students in their own assessment in ways that require them to think

about their own progress, communicate their own understanding of what they have learned, and set goals to close the gap between where they are now relative to the intended learning and where they need to be to meet standards (Chappuis et al., 2016, p. 76).

- Both teacher and students use classroom assessment information *to revise and guide* teaching and learning.

- Teachers provide students with descriptive feedback linked directly to the intended learning targets.

- Teachers keep students connected to a vision of quality as learning unfolds, continually defining for students what the learning expectations are for the lesson or unit.

One could argue that all these assessment literate teaching strategies depend on students being more involved and engaged in understanding what it is they are being asked to learn. It appears that much of what assessment for learning is all about, then, is helping students understand as clearly as possible what the learning targets are for a lesson, analyze where they are in relation to hitting those targets, and receive appropriate feedback on how to improve.

Think back to the third-grade team spotlighted in the story that started this chapter. Working together, the team members used national and state standards to clarify—within each unit of study—a set of intended outcomes for their students. Working together they settled on a task and a product—the state pamphlet—that would allow students to demonstrate mastery of those intended outcomes. However, the team forgot to communicate the intended outcomes to their students. The result was a state pamphlet project that became a frustrating and meaningless assignment for at least one student, Isabel. Because she did not have a clear picture of what it was that her teachers wanted her to learn, she wasted energy and time on a first draft that did not meet anyone's expectations for mastery.

High-performing teachers and teams at any grade level understand that the intended outcomes for a lesson must never be a secret to students. Learning-centered classrooms are built on the notion that it is imperative that students understand what is expected of them. Teachers work together to describe in student-friendly terms what proficiency with intended outcomes looks like in action. Next, they develop both a product and a process for communicating those outcomes to their students. Finally, they begin each learning cycle by saying directly to students, "This is what I want you to know—and this is how I will know if you have learned it to the level necessary to demonstrate proficiency."

The good news is that communicating essential outcomes directly to students—a research-based instructional practice that has a positive impact on student learning—does not require a significant shift in your current pedagogy. Instead, it is just going to require you to make communicating essential outcomes directly to students a daily priority.

What Can This Look Like in Your Classroom?

When collaborative teams identify exactly what their students need to learn, they work together to define the critical knowledge, skills, and dispositions each student must acquire. These prioritized learnings are also referred to as *essential outcomes, essential standards, power standards,* or *priority standards* (Jakicic, 2017). Collaborative teams then use their essential outcomes to create learning intentions and success criteria for each lesson, which help students to understand how individual activities fit into the broader context of their learning and the expectations that they must meet to "achieve success" (Hattie & Clarke, 2019, p. 57). The list of essential outcomes the team generates guides their instructional calendar. The team uses it to determine appropriate resources and pedagogical strategies for each sequence of instruction. It defines for teachers exactly what their students need to master to succeed at the next grade level. Finally, it acts as a guaranteed and viable curriculum—a curriculum that is achievable in the time available and that every teacher in the grade level or subject area agrees on, holds themselves accountable to, and carefully attends to in their individual classrooms (DuFour et al., 2016).

Teams engaged in this work are not just making a list of essential outcomes, however. Throughout the process, they engage in discussions about *why* students need to learn each essential outcome and what those outcomes look like from the students' perspective. *Why do we want our students to know or be able to do*

this? becomes an essential follow-up to the first critical question of a PLC, *What do we want our students to know and be able to do?* Identifying essential outcomes, then—a core task that is expected of every team in a PLC—*includes* talking about relevance.

When complete, the list of essential outcomes a team generates becomes a list of promises that teachers make to their students—commitments that they will pull out all the stops to fulfill. To turn them into promises, however, teams also need to ask themselves, "What will be the best format for communicating these outcomes so that students can track their level of competence independently over time?" While the answer to that question will vary depending on students' age and cognitive maturity, here are several communication practices to consider: (1) develop relevance statements for each unit of study, (2) use success checklists to guide student learning and reflection, and (3) create exemplars to make learning intentions explicit for students.

Develop Relevance Statements for Each Unit of Study

For many students, school can become tedious. Students follow the routine of learning, but they have no real sense of the answer to one simple question: *Why* are we learning this? Teacher teams that understand the negative impact this pattern can have on learners work deliberately to establish importance by connecting essential outcomes to their students' lives and ambitions. Doing so builds both motivation and engagement in learners, turning *our teaching goals* into *their learning goals.*

When establishing importance of essential outcomes and of connecting them to student lives and ambitions, the eighth-grade team at Frontier Middle School, Natrona County School District, in Casper, Wyoming, always starts by developing relevance statements for each unit (Frontier Middle School eighth-grade team, personal communication, February 22, 2010). To develop a relevance statement, the team works together to answer a series of simple questions.

- How do adults use this skill?
- When do adults use this skill?
- How are students likely to apply this skill in their academic or personal lives?

- How will mastering this skill help students to be successful both within and beyond school?

Once the team answers these questions, they craft a relevance statement written in age-appropriate language and share it with students at the beginning of the sequence of instruction. An example of a relevance statement for an interdisciplinary unit on reading functional text in middle school appears in figure 2.1.

Name of Unit: Reading Functional Text (Reading to Survive)
Start Date of Unit: February 22

Why We Are Learning This: Over the next two weeks, we will be reading a variety of everyday material, from advertisements in newspapers and maps to websites that are selling products to online reviews for restaurants in our local community. Mr. Anderson calls this kind of reading survival reading. The fancy name for it is *understanding functional text*. As we read different types of functional text, we will be reading for details, searching for solutions to problems, making predictions, uncovering clues, and drawing conclusions to make good decisions.

Ms. Stevens has found that having this skill as she reads recipes, plans her weekly grocery list, and plans her family vacations can save her money. Mr. Carlson uses this skill to build his knowledge about the way the guns he owns function and to improve his ability as a competitive target shooter. He has also found that understanding functional text like maps, websites, and online reviews helps him plan for the outdoor activities he loves—fishing, camping, and hunting.

Paying attention to details and developing the ability to cite specific information from a text to make good decisions are essential skills. At the end of the unit, you will be given an assessment that will have multiple-choice and extended-response questions.

Learning Targets:

1. I can find, cite, and explain why certain details are important to complete a task.
2. I can read a selection (pamphlet, brochure, website, recipe, policy, laws, and so on) and tell what is important and apply that information to make a good decision.

Your Summary:

Why are you learning these skills?

How will you know when you have learned these skills?

Your Self-Rating:

Use the following scale to keep track of your progress toward mastering each of the learning targets for this unit.

3	2	1
I know how to do this skill, and I can teach it to another person.	I can do this skill some of the time, but I still make mistakes and need to practice in order to get better.	I have difficulty with this skill and need help to learn how to do it correctly.

Source: © 2010 by Frontier Middle School eighth-grade team, Natrona County School District, Casper, Wyoming. Used with permission.

Figure 2.1: Relevance statement for an interdisciplinary unit on reading functional text.

Notice how the team clearly spells out exactly what functional text is for students by naming several common types of functional text—advertisements, maps, recipes, online reviews—in the relevance statement. Also, notice how the teachers include specific examples of ways they interact with functional text in their own personal lives. Both steps are designed to remind students before instruction even begins that reading functional text is not just a requirement for mastering the middle-grades curricula. Reading functional text is, instead, a skill that real people—including their teachers—use in their everyday lives.

Figure 2.2 shows another example of a relevance statement. This one was developed by a team of middle-school mathematics teachers at Frontier Middle School in Casper, Wyoming, for a unit on probability.

Again, by answering simple questions like, How do adults use this skill? and When do adults use this skill? this team moves their essential outcome—using tree diagrams to visualize probable outcomes—from a teaching goal to a goal that students see as something worth learning.

Name of Unit: Developing Tree Diagrams to Solve Probability Problems
Start Date of Unit: November 16

Why We Are Learning This: Tree diagrams are basic probability tools that can be used by statisticians, doctors, scientists, geneticists, crime solvers, fashion merchandisers, land developers, real estate investors, coaches, gamers, and even some gamblers to organize and visualize all of the possible outcomes in a sequence of events.

During the next three or four lessons, we will explore some of the different levels of the tree diagram and how you can use it in your everyday life to make calculated decisions. We have discovered it is an essential skill and one in which you must be proficient.

Learning Targets:

1. I can determine the total number of possibilities of an event from a tree diagram.
2. I will be able to read a tree diagram about probability and describe this as a ratio and relate it to a fraction.

Your Summary:

Why are you learning these skills?

How will you know when you have learned these skills?

Your Self-Rating:

Use the following scale to keep track of your progress toward mastering each of the learning targets for this unit.

3	2	1
I know how to do this skill, and I can teach it to another person.	I can do this skill some of the time, but I still make mistakes and need to practice in order to get better.	I have difficulty with this skill and need help to learn how to do it correctly.

Source: © 2010 by Frontier Middle School mathematics team, Natrona County School District, Casper, Wyoming. Used with permission.

Figure 2.2: Relevance statement for an interdisciplinary unit on probability.

Notice that both teams provide space on their relevance statements for students to summarize what they think they are supposed to be learning. This simple step allows teachers to gather feedback about the effectiveness of their relevance statements as a tool for establishing clarity around the outcomes for this sequence of instruction. Notice also that both teams include a self-rating scale that students can use to keep track of their own progress toward mastering the outcomes covered during the cycle of instruction. Doing so turns this relevance statement into the beginnings of a learning portfolio that students can refer to over the course of the year as evidence of *what* they have learned and *why* that learning matters.

Again, it is unlikely that teachers in grades preK–2 will have their students completing written relevance statements for upcoming units. However, it is just as important for preK–2 students to understand why the content and skills that they are learning matter. That means preK–2 teachers will need to find developmentally appropriate ways to structure conversations about relevance in their classrooms, too. What can those conversations look like? Teachers can integrate relevance think-alouds into their instruction, explicitly articulating places where they personally use the skills and concepts being introduced in class in their lives beyond school. Simple statements like, "Yesterday when I was baking, I used a pattern to figure out how much sugar I needed to add to my dough to make a larger batch of cookies. Isn't that neat? That's why we are studying patterns right now!" can help younger students to see that adults apply things learned in school to their lives outside of the classroom. Teachers can also ask students to find examples of characters in stories who are using concepts and skills learned in class to move themselves forward in the text. Doing so will take deliberate planning—you will have to find a collection of books where characters use the skills and concepts that you are teaching to your students—but that effort is worth it if you can convince your students from their first years in school that the things we learn in the classroom are all intentionally designed to help us succeed when faced with new situations at home.

Teacher teams interested in developing relevance statements for their next cycle of instruction can use the "Developing Relevance Statements for a Unit of Study" and "Relevance Statement for a Unit of Study" reproducibles on pages 44 and 45.

Use Success Checklists to Guide Student Learning and Reflection

John Zongker, who spent his career working at Jarrett Middle School (then Jarrett Junior High) in Springfield, Missouri, ran an amazing industrial arts program. As a special education teacher supporting students, Tim had the privilege of observing John's classroom. During any sixty-minute class period, twenty-five to thirty middle school students worked independently on different projects in his classroom. Machines of all shapes and sizes—hand saws, sanders, drill presses—whirled as students created cutting boards, screwdrivers, metal toolboxes, wooden shelves, lap desks, and cake servers. Like all middle school shop teachers, John had created a project-based learning classroom, which he did long before project-based learning became a trend in education!

While John could be characterized as old fashioned in his approach, he used instructional strategies that all of us could learn from. One of his core practices was to encourage students to take ownership of their own learning by providing a detailed success checklist for every project they were working to complete. These success checklists include a list of specific tasks for students to work through to create a successful final product. What might a success checklist look like for a junior high school industrial arts teacher? Here is a sample (see figure 2.3, page 36).

At the end of every class, John would have students clean up their work areas, put their projects away, and take out their shop notebooks. Students would then turn to the checklist for their current project. Working quietly, students checked off the things they had worked on during that period, making note of what they had completed and writing down the steps that they could take to move their project forward. Then, students started their next lesson by returning to their success checklist to set a goal for the day.

While he may not have been aware of the research supporting his practices, John's success checklists were extremely beneficial to his students. By clearly articulating the steps necessary for completing each project, he was helping his students to successfully organize and execute the actions required to produce a final product. And because students had a set of clear steps to follow as learners, they were frequently successful at creating high-quality final products. That success increased both student motivation and commitment to learning in his classroom.

Success Checklist: Wooden Cutting Board

When you buy a wooden cutting board in the store, you may not realize the multiple steps involved in creating this beautiful tool found in many kitchens. Not only is a wooden cutting board useful, but it can also be used for decoration in our homes.

In this project you will be constructing a wooden cutting board made of a variety of hardwoods. Typically, students complete this project in two weeks.

Hardwoods present some unique challenges for creating a smooth, food-safe final product. The following checklist will be your guide for creating a beautiful and functional cutting board. The quality of your project will be assessed based on not just the finished project, but by the steps you take along the way. I cannot wait to see your finished project!

Beginning Date: January 15

	Tasks to Complete	Check Off	Date Completed	Your Notes and Plans for Next Steps
1	Create a draft of the cutting board you are going to make. Be sure to include length, width, and thickness. (Your teacher must approve your plan before you begin.)			
2	Select multiple wood species of hardwood for your cutting board from the lumber storage bin.			
3	Cut wooden strips to desired width using the table saw. (Your teacher needs to supervise during this process.)			
4	Arrange the wooden strips into your desired pattern. Glue each edge using wood glue. Clamp strips together using bar clamps. Wipe away excess glue using a damp cloth and let dry.			
5	Remove excess glue using a wood scraper.			
6	Measure and cut the ends of the cutting board evenly using the table saw. Check to make sure your board is square using a carpenter's square. (Your teacher must supervise during this process.)			
7	Using the planer, gradually plane both sides of the cutting board until reaching a consistent thickness of one inch across the entire board. (Your teacher must supervise during this process.)			

8	Use the router table to round the edges of the cutting board. (Your teacher must supervise during this process.)			
9	Sand the entire board using sandpaper ranging from coarse to fine.			
10	Seal the board with food-safe mineral oil.			

After Action Report:

How successful were you at creating your cutting board? What things did you know already that helped you be successful? What things were you able to do that helped you be successful? What knowledge and skills do you still need to master to be more successful? What advice would you give a classmate who is building a cutting board?

Source: Adapted from John Zongker, 1980–1986, Jarrett Junior High, Springfield, Missouri.

Figure 2.3: Success checklist for making a cutting board in industrial arts.

Now, we know what you are thinking—there is nothing all that unique about sharing learning intentions with students. But can you spot the key difference between John's choices and the choices that many teachers make today? There are two. First, John always paired his learning intentions (making a cutting board) with a set of explicit success criteria (tasks to complete to achieve success). In his mind, learning intentions helped students to answer the question, What do I need to know? and success criteria helped students to answer the question, What do I need to be able to do? Both are essential components of the first critical question of a PLC (DuFour et al., 2016) and essential components of establishing clarity for learners (Hattie & Clarke, 2019), but many teachers forget to share explicit success criteria with their students.

John was also deliberate about engaging students in careful daily reflection about both the learning intentions and success criteria for the projects that his class was working on. Students in John's classroom used their success checklists to regularly answer three research-based questions that form the foundation of the best assessment *for* learning practices (Brookhart, 2017; Hattie, 2009; Sadler, 1998; Stiggins, Arter, Chappuis, & Chappuis, 2007).

1. Where am I going?
2. Where am I now?
3. How do I close the gap?

Of course, success checklists in primary classrooms are going to look significantly different than the success checklists for a middle school industrial arts class. First, success checklists for primary students will have far fewer steps. They are also likely to use symbols as visual cues representing key points, making it easier for developing readers to understand just what it is that their teacher expects of them. See the first-grade example in figure 2.4 (page 38).

Remember, the purpose of any success checklist is to ensure that students know exactly what it is that they need to do to be successful. Success checklists should detail for students both the learning intention (what students should know) and success criteria (what students should be able to do) for a cycle of instruction. In the primary example, by the end of the cycle of instruction, students should be able to write a complete sentence. To do so, they need to include a noun phrase, an action phrase, and an end mark in their final products.

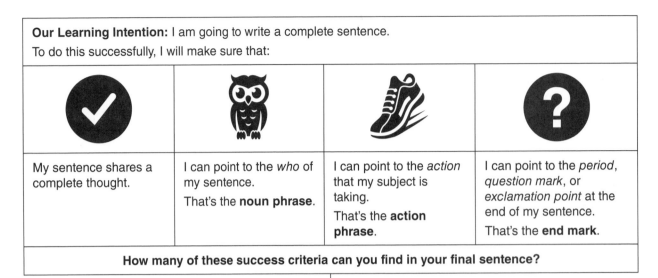

Our Learning Intention: I am going to write a complete sentence.
To do this successfully, I will make sure that:

My sentence shares a complete thought.	I can point to the *who* of my sentence. That's the **noun phrase**.	I can point to the *action* that my subject is taking. That's the **action phrase**.	I can point to the *period*, *question mark*, or *exclamation point* at the end of my sentence. That's the **end mark**.
How many of these success criteria can you find in your final sentence?			

Figure 2.4: Success checklist for grade 1.

In their groundbreaking work on evidence-based grading, Troy Gobble, Mark Onuscheck, Anthony R. Reibel, and Eric Twadell (2016) make the argument that sharing success criteria alongside learning intentions is an essential practice for ensuring student success:

> Students must be able to state what teachers are asking them to know, understand, and do. However, even clear learning targets are not enough. For those targets to be meaningful and useful learning tools, they must be scaled for proficiency expectations—in other words, we must be able to describe what proficiency looks like in terms of mastery and needs improvement. (Gobble et al., 2016, p. 4)

By creating success checklists that include both learning intentions *and* success criteria, educators can enhance students' understanding of what is expected of them. Success checklists can also help students to organize their efforts, discover learning strategies that work best for them, and abandon learning strategies that do not work. These are all behaviors that teachers in a PLC should plan for, orchestrate, and direct in their classrooms.

See the reproducible tools "Developing a Success Checklist for an Assignment" (page 46) and "Success List for a Secondary Assignment" and "Success Checklist for a Primary Assignment" on pages 47 and 48 for developing success checklists for an upcoming assignment.

Create Exemplars to Make Learning Intentions Explicit for Students

One final way that teacher teams can make learning intentions and success criteria explicit is to create sets of exemplars that they can share with their students. The idea of showing students the desired outcome for an assignment is an instructional strategy frequently found in Rick Stiggins's and Jan Chappuis's work on assessment *for* learning. Chappuis (2015) suggests that teachers share both strong and weak samples of work "to help students come to hold an understanding about accuracy and quality similar to yours before they engage in extended practice with the target" (p. 71). Doing so helps engage students, lessen ambiguity, and build confidence.

The best way for teams to create sets of exemplars is to work together to generate sample responses that highlight the strengths and weaknesses typically found in student responses at different levels of mastery (Chappuis & Stiggins, 2020). Doing so gives teams the chance to build collective clarity around the success criteria for an assignment and to share professional knowledge about the common mistakes that students are likely to make. More importantly, doing so ensures that exemplars used in the classroom are *anonymous*. Teams that use samples from their students to create exemplars risk harming the academic confidence of learners who discover their work being used by their teachers (Chappuis, 2015).

When teachers have students work with anonymous exemplars, they are also introducing an element of safety to their classrooms (Wiliam, 2016). Students are far more likely to think critically and speak openly about the weaknesses they see in anonymous work samples because they are not making judgments about their own performance or the performance of their peers. Once students can consistently spot weaknesses in anonymous work samples, they are far more likely to find and correct those same mistakes in their own work because they have a better concept of what competent performance looks like on a task (Chappuis, 2015; Chappuis & Stiggins, 2020).

For eighth-grade science teacher Paul Cancellieri, using exemplars as a tool for introducing students to the learning intentions for an assignment is a three-step process (Cancellieri, 2020a) (figure 2.5). First, Paul works with his collaborative team to develop three or four different responses to a task that students will be asked to complete or a question they will be asked to answer. The sets of exemplars that Paul's team assembles include at least one example of work that meets all expectations for mastery and two additional samples that are intentionally missing required elements for a strong final product (Cancellieri, 2020a). Creating these exemplar sets together gives Paul's team the chance to build clarity and agreement among themselves about what mastery on the required task looks like in action. Creating these exemplar sets together also gives Paul's team control over the kind and number of mistakes that they will spotlight in each exemplar. Because teachers generally know the common pitfalls students will face while completing a task or answering a question, they can design exemplars that highlight those specific pitfalls for their students (Cancellieri, 2020a).

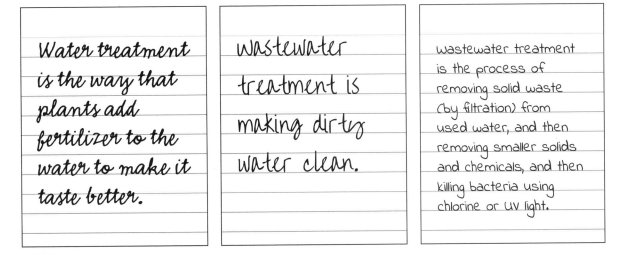

Source: Cancellieri, 2020a.

Figure 2.5: Three-step process for using exemplars to introduce students to the learning intentions for an assignment.

Next, Paul provides his students with time in class to grapple with the exemplars that his team has created (Cancellieri, 2020a). This grappling sometimes involves small groups of students working together to use the success criteria for an assignment to rank exemplars in order from best to worst. Other times, it involves those same small groups sorting exemplars into categories based on the success criteria that they include or that they are missing (Cancellieri, 2020a). Paul could also provide students with several sample feedback comments and ask students to match the feedback comments with the exemplar that they are designed to support (Wiliam, 2016). Throughout these exemplar exploration activities, Paul repeatedly asks students and groups to defend the sorting decisions that they are making. Doing so allows him to be sure that his students can articulate meaningful differences between strong and weak responses to the assignment that they are working on (Cancellieri, 2020a). Doing so also requires students to look closely at each exemplar to determine its individual strengths and weaknesses. This kind of close examination is essential for building a student's understanding of the success criteria for individual assignments (Cancellieri, 2020a).

The final step Paul takes when using exemplars to introduce his students to learning intentions is to work with his classes to create a single-point rubric for the task they are completing or the question they are being asked to answer (Cancellieri, 2020a) (figure 2.6). Single-point rubrics describe only what *meeting* grade-level expectations looks like. By developing the single-point scoring rubric together after examining exemplars, students are working to articulate the

success criteria essential for demonstrating mastery on the upcoming assignment. And by asking students to develop success criteria after looking at exemplars, Paul is setting his students up with both the information and the language necessary to accurately evaluate their own performance on the exact same task (Cancellieri, 2020a). As Hattie and Clarke (2019) explain, "When success criteria are co-constructed with students, rather than simply given to them, students have a still greater chance of understanding and internalizing their meanings and possessing a concept of the goal" (pp. 57–58).

What NEEDS TO IMPROVE to Meet Expectations?	MASTERY	What Went BEYOND Expectations?
	☐ Completely answers the question. ☐ Provides the correct answer. ☐ Explains the steps in the right order.	

Source: Cancellieri, 2020a.

Figure 2.6: Sample single-point rubric.

Paul is deliberate about using single-point rubrics with his students because they limit the amount of information that students need to consider when trying to understand the learning intentions and success criteria for an assignment (Cancellieri, 2020a). Unlike more traditional rubrics, single-point rubrics only describe what *meeting* grade-level expectations looks like in action. This is important when building students' evaluative capacity because it keeps their efforts focused on a small handful of steps that they can take to move their learning forward. When students are given *more information* about different levels of mastery on a particular task, you are likely to see them take *less action* to improve their own work because they are overwhelmed by trying to understand your expectations for the assignment (Cancellieri, 2020b; Shute, 2007). The single-point rubrics that Paul and his students create together give students information that "is just in time, just for them, just for where they are in their learning process, and just what they need to move forward" (Hattie, 2012, p. 19).

It is important to note that the exemplar sets teams create for students to grapple with *do not have to be*

text based. A team of art teachers could use drawings or sculptures as exemplars, a team of band directors could use audio recordings of musical performances as exemplars, and a team of primary teachers could use video demonstrations of performance tasks—using phonics strategies correctly, applying steps in mathematics problems appropriately, accurately sorting sets of items to identify patterns—as exemplars. That means any team—regardless of the subject or grade level that they teach—can use exemplars to introduce their students to the learning intentions and success criteria for an assignment. The key to a good set of exemplars is simply to choose a format—text, pictures, audio, recordings—that most closely resembles the work products that students are being asked to create.

Working with exemplars helps students realize that there *are* success criteria for every task. Working with exemplars also gives students chances to look for those success criteria in work they examine. Finally, working with exemplars leaves students convinced that they have what it takes to apply their knowledge of success criteria to both produce and evaluate their own performances.

You can find a template to use to develop exemplars with your collaborative team, "Developing Exemplars to Make Learning Intentions Explicit," on page 49 and a template "Developing a Set of Exemplars to Make Learning Intentions Explicit" on page 50. You can also find a tool for creating a single-point rubric, "Developing a Single-Point Rubric With Your Students," on page 51.

Recommendations for Getting Started

Identifying a small set of essential outcomes to focus on during each unit of instruction is a common practice for collaborative teams in a PLC. We believe that if you are already doing this work with one another, you can quickly point to sets of prioritized learning intentions that are already written in student-friendly language and that you are posting on the board at the beginning of each lesson.

But remember, if learning intentions and success criteria are to have a positive impact on students as learners, they must become something more than just words written on your board; they must become targets that are clearly understood by and communicated to everyone—teachers, parents, *and* students. More important, they must become targets that students believe are both worthwhile and achievable. To make that happen, we suggest the following actions: (1) ask students for feedback, (2) be patient with students, and (3) encourage teams to develop their own best practices.

Ask Students for Feedback

This chapter began with the story of Isabel, a third grader determined to do well in class, but unsure of exactly what the state pamphlet that she had been assigned was supposed to look like. Like most students, Isabel did her best. But in the end, she needed significant support from her mother to produce a pamphlet that she could be proud of. Imagine how frustrating that must have been for *everyone*. Isabel probably worried that her final product would disappoint both her parents and her teacher. Isabel's mother probably dropped everything to help her daughter to finish an ambiguous task at the last minute. Isabel's teacher probably ended up with several final products from other confused students that did not meet grade-level expectations, causing him to spend time reteaching skills that he thought his students had already learned.

All this frustration could have been prevented if Isabel's teacher had taken time to learn from his students *during* the instructional cycle. Had he asked students to explain the outcomes and expectations for the state pamphlet project any time before they turned in their final products, he would have discovered that his students did not have enough clarity to meet his expectations. Hattie (2009) describes this preassignment action as gathering feedback from—rather than giving feedback to—students, and he argues that it is an essential element of good teaching:

> I discovered that feedback is most powerful when it is from the student to the teacher. What they know, what they understand, where they make errors, when they have misconceptions, when they are not engaged—then teaching and learning can be synchronized and powerful. Feedback to teachers makes learning visible. (p. 173)

What does this mean for classroom teachers? It means that we cannot assume that students understand the purpose of the tasks that we are assigning simply because we have shared a learning target with them in student-friendly language. Instead, to gather feedback on whether students understand the purpose of tasks, we must intentionally ask them to explain why they are completing assignments and how those assignments will move their learning forward (Chappuis & Stiggins, 2020). Stated another way, establishing clarity in our classrooms depends first on understanding just what it is that our students *think* they are supposed to be learning.

Be Patient With Students

For most students, articulating the reasons that learning intentions are essential, setting daily goals from success checklists, and using exemplars to identify the characteristics of both high- and low-quality work are new behaviors that they have never been asked to demonstrate in an academic setting. This means your early efforts to help students better understand the expectations that you are asking them to master might feel like failed attempts at good instruction. You might have students who seem disengaged in lessons, you might hear groans when you ask students to take out their success checklists at the beginning of every class period, and you might notice that even with coaching and support, students struggle to use exemplars as tools for improving their final products.

In those moments, it is important to be patient. Remember that by deliberately encouraging students to wrestle with a question that typically only teachers answer—What should students know and be able to do by the end of a unit of instruction?—you are disrupting the regular routine of schools. Students will not automatically be able to identify the relevance in your learning intentions because they have never been asked to think about relevance before. Measuring progress against success checklists will not come naturally to students because they are used to being assessed in every circumstance by the adults in their lives. Using exemplars to define what mastery looks like in action will feel foreign to students who have always been told what to include in their final products—and who have always been corrected by teachers when those criteria are missing.

Over time and with persistence, you will establish new patterns in your classroom. No longer will students see themselves as passive participants in learning. Instead, they will recognize that they have both the skills and ability to understand the expectations for the lessons they are learning each day. And, more important, they will recognize that learners always play an active role in tracking their own progress toward mastery. These outcomes are worth waiting for.

Encourage Teams to Develop Their Own Best Practices

Finally, a reminder for school leaders: As collaborative teams design strategies to help students understand the expectations for a cycle of instruction, remember that their conversations around what works best for students are as valuable as any product they may create. We have seen scenarios where well-intentioned school leaders are introduced to products shared at conferences or in professional development sessions and then mandate that teachers in every classroom across their schools use a *single format* for building relevance into their classroom practice.

We do not suggest a one-size-fits-all approach. Instead, we suggest that school leaders create an environment of autonomy with accountability (Pink, 2009). We believe that it is fine for school leaders to make developing self-efficacy in learners a priority in their buildings and to hold teams accountable for demonstrating how that work is being done, but that teacher teams should have the freedom and flexibility to experiment and develop methods and instruments based on their understanding of the thinking and processing skills of their students. Stated another way, the key is not that every team in a building uses the same template to engage students in a study of the outcomes they are expected to master. The key is that every team recognizes the importance of empowering students as partners in the learning process and that every team is convinced of their ability to design learning experiences that have a positive impact on student success.

Concluding Thoughts

Setting aside instructional time to introduce students to the relevance of the learning intentions they are being asked to master, giving students chances to reflect on the specific steps they must take to demonstrate mastery of those learning intentions, and asking students to spot success criteria in exemplars are all great strategies for building clarity in learners. Students are empowered in classrooms where teachers share learning intentions and success criteria transparently because they can set goals for themselves and better judge their progress relative to teacher expectations (Brookhart, 2017; Chappuis, 2015; Chappuis & Stiggins, 2020; Ruiz-Primo & Brookhart, 2018).

Having conversations within collaborative teams about how to best communicate expectations to students is equally important because those conversations ensure that all the teachers at a grade level or in a subject area have a *shared understanding* of what proficient learners should know and be able to do. At first glance, this may seem like a no-brainer. Of course, teachers should have a shared understanding of what proficient students should know and be able to do. That is not always the case, however. State and national standards documents are often written in complex language that is difficult to understand or easy to misinterpret. What is more, even if teachers who are working in the same subject or grade level have a shared understanding of a learning standard, they may prioritize different success criteria when determining whether students are meeting grade-level expectations.

The solution is simple: Work with colleagues whenever you are developing plans to help students understand expectations for a cycle of instruction. Conversations with peers about what standards mean, why standards matter, and what grade-level mastery of standards looks like are valuable learning opportunities for educators (DuFour et al., 2016). Teams that develop relevance statements, success checklists, and sets of exemplars together build clarity around just what students are supposed to know and be able to do—and that clarity increases the likelihood that any instruction teams plan, assessment they develop, and curriculum material they choose will actually advance learning (Ainsworth, 2017).

Developing Relevance Statements for a Unit of Study

Helping students find value in education is an essential first step toward engaging them as full partners in the learning process. Answer the following questions below with your learning team to develop a shared answer to the question that every student has at the beginning of a unit of study: *Why do we have to learn this?*

Name of Unit:	
Essential Concepts and Skills Covered During This Unit:	

Questions to Consider	Your Team's Response
How do adults use these concepts and skills? When do adults use these concepts and skills? How do the teachers on your team use these concepts and skills? How do other influential adults in your school community use these concepts and skills?	
Where are students likely to apply these skills in their academic lives? Where are students likely to apply these skills in their personal lives?	
How will mastering these skills help students be successful both within and beyond school?	

Now, use the tool on page 45 to craft a short relevance statement that you can share with students at the beginning of your next unit of instruction. Remember that a good relevance statement should:

Be written in student-friendly language

Include specific examples of ways that students will use essential concepts and skills in their everyday life

Leave space for students to both summarize what they are supposed to be learning and to rate the progress they are making toward mastery

Relevance Statement for a Unit of Study

Over the next few weeks, we will be working through a new unit of study. This relevance statement is designed to help you better understand why learning these concepts and skills matters to YOU. It also gives you a space to track your progress toward learning the essential concepts and skills during this unit.

Student Name:

Name of Unit: _____ Start Date of Unit: _____

Why We Are Learning This:

Learning Targets to Master:

Your Summary: Now that you have read the relevance statement your teachers have created, use the two questions below to craft a summary about why these concepts and skills are important to learn.

1. Why are you learning these skills?
2. How will you know when you have learned these skills?

Your Self-Rating:

Use the scale below to keep track of your progress toward mastering each of the learning targets for this unit.

1	2	3
I have difficulty understanding these concepts or knowing how to do these skills and need help to learn how to do them correctly.	I understand these concepts and know how to do these skills some of the time, but I still make mistakes and need to practice to get better.	I understand these concepts and know how to do these skills, and I can teach them to another person.

Developing a Success Checklist for an Assignment

Another essential step toward engaging students as full partners in the learning process is explicitly defining the steps that students need to take to demonstrate mastery on an assignment and then sharing those steps with students on success checklists that they can refer to during the course of instruction. Answer the questions that follow with your collaborative team to begin developing a success checklist for an upcoming assignment.

Name of Assignment:	
Questions to Consider	**Your Team's Response**
What kinds of things should students know by the time that they are done with this assignment?	
What kinds of things should students be able to do by the time that they are done with this assignment?	
Is there a logical progression that students should follow when completing this assignment? What should they do first? What should they do second? What should they do third?	
What are the common mistakes that we see students making when working on this assignment? Why do they make those mistakes?	

Now, use the template on page 47 to craft a success checklist that you can share with students at the beginning of your assignment. Remember that a good success checklist should:

- Be written in student-friendly language
- Include both a description of what students should know by the end of an assignment and a specific set of success criteria detailing things that students should be able to do to meet their teacher's expectations
- Have space for students to record reflections on their progress toward mastery

Success Checklist for a Secondary Assignment

Over the next few weeks, we will be working on a new assignment. This success checklist is designed to help you monitor your progress toward meeting the expectations for the assignment. It also gives you a space to record reflections and set goals for yourself. We will revisit this checklist regularly while working on this assignment.

Name of Assignment:

Explanation of Assignment:

Tasks to Complete	Your Notes

Final Reflection:

How successful were you at completing this assignment? What things did you know that helped you be successful? What things were you able to do that helped you be successful? What knowledge or skills do you still need to master to be more successful?

Success Checklist for a Primary Assignment

It is time for us to learn something new together! Here is a checklist you can use to see how you are doing as a learner. Remember to use the pictures on our success checklist as a reminder of what we should be able to see in your work!

Our Learning Intention:				
To do this successfully, I will make sure that:				
Picture Cues				
Word Cues				
How many of these success criteria can you find in your final product?				

Developing Exemplars to Make Learning Intentions Explicit

Providing students with exemplars of final products is a valuable practice because it allows students to see what learning intentions and success criteria for assignments look like in action. When students can spot success criteria—or lack thereof—in exemplars, they are better prepared to spot those same criteria in their own work. Answer the questions below with your learning team to develop a set of exemplars for an upcoming task that you are going to ask students to complete.

Name of Assignment:
Essential Concepts and Skills Covered During This Assignment:

Questions to Consider	Your Team's Response
Name up to three elements you expect to find in a final product that met your team's expectations for proficiency on this assignment.	
Name up to three elements you expect to find in a final product that went beyond your team's expectations for proficiency on this assignment.	
What kind of mistakes do students who are struggling to demonstrate proficiency typically make on this assignment?	

Now, use the template on page 50 to craft a set of exemplars for this assignment. Remember that a good set of exemplars should:

- Include at least two different examples designed to highlight varying levels of student performance
- Be teacher-created samples designed to illustrate both success criteria and common mistakes found frequently in student work
- Include an opportunity for students to compare their own work to the exemplars they studied

Developing a Set of Exemplars to Make Learning Intentions Explicit

Use this template to develop a set of exemplars for one of your upcoming tasks. Remember that you will need to fill out one template for each level of performance that you want to highlight in your set of exemplars.

Task students will complete or question students will answer to demonstrate mastery:

Learning target task is designed to assess (written in student-friendly language):

Level of performance this exemplar demonstrates (circle one):			
Beginning	Developing	Mastering	Exceeding
Exemplar (Team generates to deliberately spotlight common patterns seen in student responses at this level of performance)		**Teacher comments** (Detail the reasons that this exemplar is an accurate representation of responses at this level of performance.)	

Defining characteristics of responses demonstrating this level of performance (a one- or two-sentence summary written in student-friendly language):

Source: Ferriter, W. M. (2020). The big book of tools for collaborative teams in a PLC at Work (p. 64). Bloomington, IN: Solution Tree Press.

Developing a Single-Point Rubric With Your Students

Remember that single-point rubrics should be developed together with your students after they have had the chance to grapple with a set of exemplars designed to highlight both the success criteria and common mistakes found in student responses to classroom tasks (Cancellieri, 2020a). To develop a single-point rubric with your students, consider projecting this template onto your classroom whiteboard and then leading a classroom discussion around the following questions.

1. What kinds of things would we see in a successful student response to this question or assignment?

2. If a student were struggling with this question or assignment, what kinds of mistakes would they make?

3. Are there any basics or *fundamentals*—things like proper grammar in writing or accurate calculations in mathematics—that we would expect students to demonstrate consistently when answering questions or completing assignments like this?

As you spot trends in student responses during your classroom discussion, begin crafting the success criteria for the assignment in the center column of the following table. When you think all important success criteria have been identified, ask students to vote on the criteria statements that you have crafted. Allow any student who feels that essential criteria have been left out of your statements to share his or her thinking with the class.

Areas Where You Could Improve Your Work	Criteria for the Assignment	Areas Where You Went Beyond Expectations

page 1 of 2

Areas Where You Could Improve Your Work	Criteria for the Assignment	Areas Where You Went Beyond Expectations

*Source: Cancellieri, P. (2020a, June 11). Creating a culture of feedback book study: Session two—How am I doing? [Video file].
Accessed at https://solutiontree.wistia.com/medias/ra3371pryg on June 27, 2020.*

3 Helping Students Assess Their Progress Toward Mastery

Maddie, a student in coauthor Bill Ferriter's sixth-grade science classroom, was evaluating her own conclusion for a lab report by comparing it to two exemplars that Bill had provided to every student. While working, Maddie successfully analyzed both exemplars, identifying the strengths and weaknesses commonly found in student conclusions and explaining the impact that those strengths and weaknesses have on student writing. Then, she returned to her lab report and improved it based on what she had learned from her analysis of the exemplars. As a result, her final product was one of the strongest student conclusions Bill had ever seen.

Later that week, Bill and Maddie sat together and talked through the entire experience. When Bill asked Maddie about her conclusion, Maddie pointed out several things she thought she had done well, changes she made to her work after examining the exemplars Bill had provided, and plans she had for improving her conclusions in the future. Throughout the entire conversation, Maddie showed insight about her strengths and weaknesses that confirmed to Bill that his work to integrate student self-assessment into his instructional plans was paying off. It was clear that Maddie understood that *she* had the ability to close the gap between where she currently was as a learner and where she wanted to be—and it was clear that she was ready to take action to move herself forward.

But then Maddie asked a question. "Yes, Mr. Ferriter," she said, "but what's my grade on this assignment?"

Maddie's question caught Bill by surprise. After all, they had just spent ten minutes talking about her performance together, and Maddie clearly understood both her strengths and weaknesses when it came to writing a conclusion for a lab report. If anyone knew how to rate the quality of a conclusion, it was Maddie, and she had just finished proving that to both herself and her teacher.

To those who have worked with older students in schools, Maddie's question is anything but surprising. Maddie—like most sixth graders—has already learned to play the game of school. In this game, teachers assign tasks, students complete tasks, and teachers grade tasks. This well-worn pattern repeated in classroom after classroom with teacher after teacher on assignment after assignment has cemented in Maddie's mind the notion that the final word on student performance belongs to the teacher who expresses it as a grade in the gradebook. Maddie's question is not evidence of a student *who needed a grade* to know whether she had achieved mastery. Instead, Maddie's question is evidence of a student *who believed that she needed a grade* to know whether she had achieved mastery because a grade is a teacher's opinion on performance, and a teacher's opinion on performance *always* means more than a student's does.

For collaborative teams, the second critical question of learning in a PLC—How will we know if students are learning?—is formulated with adults in mind. Teams collect evidence of student progress for two reasons. First, they collect evidence of student progress because team members accept responsibility for helping *all* students master *every* outcome the team has identified as essential—and without carefully tracking progress by both student and standard, meeting that goal is impossible. Second, teams collect evidence of student progress because that evidence can help members identify instructional practices that are working and instructional practices that teachers should abandon. Both of those behaviors are foundational to the work of any group of teachers in a PLC.

We argue that it is just as important for *students* to be able to answer the question, How will I know if I am learning? Regular opportunities for self-assessment provide students with greater ownership over—and a deeper connection to—their current levels of proficiency. Regular opportunities for self-assessment also change the view that students hold of both themselves and of their role in the learning process. Teams that design regular opportunities for self-assessment activate their students as full partners in the assessment process. Finally, teams that design regular opportunities for self-assessment naturally lead students to discovering answers to the third and fourth critical questions of a PLC: What steps should I take when I am struggling to master important outcomes? and How can I extend my learning after I have mastered important outcomes? We will share strategies to address questions three and four in chapter 4.

For now, let's examine why it is important for students to engage in processes that help them accurately reflect on their own progress.

Why Is This Important to Learners?

Here is a question to consider. On a scale from one to five—where one represents "not very" and five represents "incredibly"—how *important* do you think it is for students to be able to assess their own progress toward mastery? Chances are, you already believe that self-assessment is an essential behavior that all students should master. Now, a second question. On a scale from one to five—where one represents "once in a while" and five represents "every lesson, every day"—how *frequently* do you give students chances to assess their own progress toward mastery?

Bill has asked his students questions like these for years, and for years, his students have told him that they are *rarely* asked to assess their own progress toward mastery. This causes us great concern. If we are ever going to move from a culture of teaching and grading in schools to a culture of learning, teachers must become skilled at turning their students into capable partners in the assessment process. Remember, assessments "should provide students with information about how to advance their understanding of content and teachers with information about how to help students do so" (Marzano, 2017, p. 44). As Chappuis and Stiggins (2020) explain, formative assessment is most powerful when *students* are "examining, interpreting, and acting" (p. 6) on information about their own performance. It is impossible to develop students who can advance their understanding of content if we never ask them *to evaluate their own performance* on the assessments we are using in our instruction.

This argument—that students must become active partners in the assessment process—has been confirmed again and again by experts in the field of education. For example, educational researchers Paul Black and Dylan Wiliam first suggested in the late 1990s that improving learning through assessment depends on "five deceptively simple, key factors."

1. The provision of effective feedback to students

2. The active involvement of students in their own learning

3. Adjusting teaching to take account of the results of assessment

4. A recognition of the profound influence assessment has on the motivation and self-esteem of students, both of which are crucial influences on learning

5. The need for students to be able to assess themselves and understand how to improve (as cited in Hattie & Clarke, 2019, p. 9)

Many of these deceptively simple, key factors appear again in the work of Connie Moss and Susan Brookhart (2019), who remind readers that "if students are not intentionally gathering and using evidence from their own work to improve their learning, then what is happening does not meet our definition of formative assessment" (p. 7). For Moss and Brookhart, teachers help students to intentionally gather and use evidence to improve their own learning whenever they:

1. Articulate clear learning targets to students and explicitly describe what mastery looks like.

2. Provide targeted feedback with the intention of furthering learning.

3. Teach students to use success criteria to assess their own learning.

4. Help students to set clearly defined goals for themselves—and then adjust their next moves based both on feedback given by teachers and gathered from the learning environment.

5. Use targeted questioning to promote formative discourse (Moss & Brookhart, 2019).

Teachers in PLCs know that improving learning through assessment begins by writing common formative assessments. DuFour and DuFour (2012) suggest that common formative assessments are essential in a PLC because they do the following:

1. Inform each teacher of individual students who need intervention because they are struggling to learn or of students who need enrichment because they are already proficient

2. Inform students of the next steps they must take in their learning

3. Inform each member of the team of his or her individual strengths and weaknesses in teaching particular skills so each member can provide or solicit help from colleagues on the team

4. Inform the team of areas where many students are struggling so that the team can develop and implement better strategies for teaching those areas (p. 41)

Notice that all three sets of experts contend that *engaging students* is a critical element to improving learning through assessment. In fact, when important adults—teachers, parents, coaches—are the

sole assessors of performance, students "become increasingly insecure about their own judgment and dependent on the advice of experts" (Wiggins, 2012, p. 12). "What we need," suggest Nancy Frey, John Hattie, and Douglas Fisher (2018), "are learners who understand their current performance, recognize the gap between their current performance and the expected performance, and select strategies to close that gap" (p. 12).

Activating students as partners in the assessment process ensures that classrooms become feedback-rich environments. In classrooms where teachers are the only providers of feedback, students must wait to learn about their individual successes and struggles (Wiliam, 2016). That wait can take a long time, depending on the number of students an individual teacher is responsible for supporting. In classrooms where students are taught to accurately evaluate their own performance, however, feedback can be both timely and directive, essential characteristics of assessment that improve learning (Marzano, 2017). That means the need for pupils to be able to assess themselves and understand how to improve should not be viewed as an extra in classrooms, but rather as an integral part of the planning and intentional design of every lesson.

It is important to note that self-assessment practices—like the mission and vision building practices discussed in chapter 1—must be introduced early in a student's educational journey. After all, from their first days in the classroom, students are developing notions about their ability as learners based on the feedback they receive. Grades—which remain the most common type of feedback given to learners of all ages—signal to students that a final decision has been made about their learning (Hattie & Clarke, 2019). For students who struggle, the emotional response to lots of poor marks—particularly those given with no clear pathway to improvement—can have a long-lasting, negative impact on both motivation and engagement (Schinske & Tanner, 2014).

When students are taught early on to assess their own progress, however, they quickly find evidence that they *are* capable and competent learners. That belief in evidence has a dramatic effect on each student's sense of self-efficacy (Chappuis & Stiggins, 2020; Hattie & Clarke, 2019). Once students become convinced that they *can* be successful in school, they are more likely to take risks and to work with their teachers to set goals and develop action steps that will help them to improve (Moss & Brookhart, 2019).

Can you see what is happening here? Confident learners are persistent—and persistent learners are successful. How successful? In his research on the in-school practices we use that have the greatest impact on student achievement, Hattie (2017) notes that self-reporting grades—the process of asking students to predict how they will do on an assignment and then proving to them that they have the ability to go beyond even their own expectations—is the highest-leverage pedagogical strategy that teachers can implement in their classrooms. As Hattie explains:

> If I was redoing it again, I'd probably relabel self-reported grades as student expectations because that's really what they are—the expectations students set for their work. And my major and loud message is that . . . we need to raise those expectations and give the students the confidence and the skills and the understandings that they can exceed. (Cognition Education, 2012)

Now turn that around and think about students who go through school without ever finding evidence that they can exceed their own expectations. Earning the same marks over and over again on task after task, students begin to define themselves by the letters and numbers that we assign to them—and those definitions can cause students to give up on learning by the time they reach middle and high school. We see the impact of this kind of self-definition in the students who check out at the beginning of every class, putting their heads down or their hoods up from the moment that they walk through the door. We also see the impact of those self-definitions in students who complete little—if any—work. And while those behaviors are frustrating to classroom teachers, they are not surprising. Why, after all, should struggling students lean in on challenging tasks when they already know in advance what grade they are probably going to earn?

This chapter is not just an argument for instructional practices that have a higher than ordinary impact on student achievement. The foundation of this chapter is the moral imperative that educators find ways to "use classroom assessment practices

to either (1) Keep all learners from losing hope to begin with or (2) Rebuild that hope once it has been destroyed" (Stiggins & Chappuis, 2005, p. 12).

What Can This Look Like in Your Classroom?

Our guess is that you *already know* what good formative assessment looks like. Good formative assessment is happening in the following scenarios.

- A high school drafting teacher who is helping students to use an AutoCAD program to develop a three-dimensional layout for kitchen cabinets stops his instructional sequence, gives a quiz, and plans a set of next steps targeting the needs of both his whole class and small groups of students based on the evidence that he finds in the results of the quiz.

- A middle school family and consumer science teacher ends her class five minutes before the dismissal bell and asks all students to use an index card as an exit ticket to list five reasons why prenatal care is critical to the health of a baby and five reasons why it is critical to the health of the mother. Reviewing student responses later that day, the teacher notices that most of her students completed this task with ease. Realizing that the pedagogical strategy she used for this lesson was effective, she then considers ways that she can duplicate it as she plans instruction for the next essential outcome in her current unit of study.

- An elementary mathematics teacher passes out small whiteboards and markers and asks students to work out problems and processes. Each time students finish a problem, they show their whiteboards to the teacher—who then asks one or two students to explain how they arrived at their answers. Looking for common patterns in both the solutions and explanations that students share for each question allows the teacher to develop a sense for how his students are thinking about mathematics, information that will help him as he designs lessons for the next school day.

Why is each of these scenarios an example of good formative assessment? Because formative assessments—the questions that we ask and the tasks that we use to continuously gather evidence during a sequence of instruction about the progress students are making toward mastery—are designed to *inform our next actions* (DuFour et al., 2016). Teachers should use formative assessments to identify students who need intervention or extension, identify pedagogical strategies that are worth replicating (or that should be abandoned), and adjust instructional plans (DuFour et al., 2016). Each of the simple practices in the previous bulleted list gave teachers valuable information about both their students and their lessons—information that teachers can then use to immediately improve their practice and help more students learn at higher levels.

What is missing from each of these scenarios? None of the examples give students the chance to assess their own progress toward mastery—a critical element of any attempt to use assessment to improve learning (Brookhart, 2017; Chappuis & Stiggins, 2020; DuFour et al., 2016; Moss & Brookhart, 2019). As Chappuis and Stiggins (2020) explain, "The student is an equally important decision maker *whose information needs must be met* during the learning as well. In our experience, student needs get lost in the formative assessment picture because it centers so heavily on teacher's needs" (p. 7, emphasis in original). What does this all mean? While all teachers and collaborative teams should be applauded for using embedded formative assessments to reflect on their *teaching*, it is equally important to design opportunities for students to use embedded formative assessment to reflect on their *learning* (Chappuis & Stiggins, 2020; Hattie, 2011; Marzano, 2017). We present three strategies teachers can use to make that shift in the classroom: (1) have students reflect on and rework their mistakes, (2) provide regular opportunities for short-term goal setting, and (3) have students keep a record of their progress.

Have Students Reflect on and Rework Their Mistakes

Leah Alcala, a seventh- and eighth-grade mathematics teacher at King Middle School in Berkeley, California, noticed an all-too-familiar pattern when handing back graded papers to her students. "What I was finding when handing back tests the old way

where I put a grade on it," she explains, "was kids would look at their grade, decide whether they were good at math or not, and put the test away and never look at it again" (Alcala, n.d.). So, she decided to rethink the way that she both scores and returns papers to her students as a start to rebuilding their capacity for self-assessment. Now, after giving a test in class, Leah goes through all the papers that she collects, highlighting mistakes she finds. Those highlights are the *only* feedback she gives to students when she returns their work (Alcala, n.d.). There are no grades or written comments on student papers at all.

Her next step is to guide students through conversations about what she calls her "favorite mistakes" before handing back papers (Alcala, n.d.). She chooses these mistakes by looking for common errors while reviewing student work. Then, she takes pictures of them and shares them with her students in class on the day that her tests are scheduled to be returned. Students work in small groups to figure out what errors were made in Leah's favorite mistakes and how to best correct them (Alcala, n.d.). "It becomes a part of the classwork of getting a test back," Alcala explains, "to figure out why they made a mistake in this particular step" (Alcala, n.d.).

Once the class has reviewed her favorite mistakes, she hands tests back to her students and asks them to review the highlights on their own papers. Because the class has already spent time talking through the reasoning behind the most common errors on the test, students are well prepared to assess both the progress they made toward mastering outcomes and the steps they still need to take to improve their practice (Alcala, n.d.). Leah does give students traditional grades on every test, but she does not post those grades in her online gradebook until the day after the test. Doing so gives students the time to study their mistakes and make corrections in preparation for retesting. "By not putting a grade on the test, I feel like what I'm allowing them to do is wrestle with the math that they produced for me first and think of the grade second," Leah says. "My hope is that through this strategy, they see that studying their mistakes and learning from their mistakes is really what learning is" (Alcala, n.d.).

What Leah has done is turn feedback into detective work—a process that Dylan Wiliam (2015) argues is an essential characteristic of assessment that improves learning. "The first fundamental principle of effective classroom feedback," Wiliam (2011) explains, "is that feedback should be more work for the recipient than the donor" (Location No. 2617). By highlighting errors and reviewing favorite mistakes with the whole class, Leah has given students enough information to correct their own mistakes, but not so much information that students are robbed of the opportunity to assess themselves accurately.

Leah could add to her strategy by asking students to complete a rework plan after reviewing the highlights on their test papers. Rework plans are simple templates that encourage students to take immediate action to improve their learning on one specific task. Rework plans are also useful tools for developing assessment capacity in learners because students can use their first attempts to find evidence of the specific changes that they need to make to improve their current levels of mastery (Chappuis & Stiggins, 2020). Once they have completed reworks, students can compare their final attempts to their initial work "to show themselves and others how far they have come, even if they have not yet fully attained their stated goals" (Stiggins et al., 2007, p. 368).

While primary teachers are unlikely to have their students completing written rework plans for important assessments or assignments, it is just as essential for young learners to get into the habit of seeing their initial attempts at learning as first drafts that can be improved on and to realize that they have the skills necessary to move their work forward. Encouraging the development of these habits in the primary classroom can be as simple as using opening questions—*What did you struggle with on your first attempt at this assignment?, What steps would you take to correct the mistakes that you made on your initial attempt at this assignment?, Where will you turn if you need help?, and When will your rework be finished?*—in informal conversations and formal conferences with students after important tasks have been completed. The goal of rework planning in the primary classroom is not to have students create a written plan that they can refer to or review with their parents. Instead, the goal of rework planning in the primary classroom is to both introduce and reinforce the notion that planning next steps is something that every learner does when reflecting on his or her current levels of mastery.

Figure 3.1 shows a sample rework planning template to use with students.

Can you see how this rework planning template is an example of turning feedback into detective work? The questions in the left column are intentionally designed to "help students harness the workings of their own minds"(Moss & Brookhart, 2019)—a critical element of well-designed opportunities for formative discourse. Through questioning, students are asked to think deliberately about the success criteria of the assignment, about how their own work compares to those success criteria, and about steps that can be taken to seek out help or to make corrections to their first attempts. As students work to answer the strategic questions asked on a rework planning template and to create an improved final product, they are developing the self-regulation behaviors—attending to expectations, knowing when to ask questions, collecting information about progress, setting realistic and attainable goals—necessary for taking ownership over their own learning (Moss & Brookhart, 2019).

If you are interested in using rework planning templates with your students, you can find a blank, reproducible version of this template on page 71.

Provide Regular Opportunities for Short-Term Goal Setting

Another simple step collaborative teams can take to build capacity for self-assessment is to give students lots of opportunities to set and achieve meaningful learning goals. Goal setting is a logical practice for teams interested in integrating self-assessment into their instruction because it requires students to think critically about their current levels of mastery, develop an action plan for moving themselves forward, and collect evidence to document the progress that they are making (Chappuis, 2015; Chappuis & Stiggins, 2020; Moss & Brookhart, 2019). Collaborative teams in PLCs already understand the power of goal setting. After all, collaborative teams in PLCs work interdependently to achieve a common goal for which they hold themselves mutually accountable (DuFour et al., 2016). The goals that collaborative teams work toward together in PLCs are strategic and specific, measurable, attainable, results oriented, and time bound (Conzemius & O'Neill, 2014), and the commitment of teams to work to accomplish these SMART goals will ultimately move learning forward in their

Student Name:	
Directions: To raise your score on your recent test or project, you must use this tool to develop and then complete a rework plan. When you have completed your rework plan, please have it signed by both your teacher and your parents.	
Name of assignment you are reworking: My Claim, Evidence, Reasoning Paragraph on Pathogens	

Questions to Consider	Your Response
What did you struggle with on your initial attempt at this assignment? Were there things that you did not know? Things that you were not sure how to do? Did you make any of the common mistakes that we reviewed in class? Which ones?	On my initial attempt at writing a claim, evidence, reasoning paragraph on which pathogen that we studied is the most dangerous, I struggled with writing good reasoning sentences. This was one of the common mistakes that we studied in class. Like other students, my reasoning sentences didn't explain how the facts that I included supported the claim that I was making. Most of the time, I just listed more facts.
What steps will you take to correct the mistakes that you made on your initial attempt at this assignment? Are there concepts that you need to review again? Do you need some extra practice problems? Will you attend a review session or find a classmate to lend a hand?	I am going to look back at the sample "mistakes" shared in class—and the corrections to those mistakes first. Then, I'm going to revise my original sentences. To see if I really understand the difference between reasoning sentences and evidence, I am going to complete the practice set that you handed out in class today. I will come to working lunch to get it checked.
Where will you turn if you need help? What resources are available to you to help you correct your mistakes? Is your teacher offering a rework session? Do you have a classmate that can lend a hand? Are there resources like textbooks or handouts that can help?	My friend Thomas told me that he got all of his reasoning sentences right, so I can ask him to look at my revisions before I turn them in.
When will your rework be finished?	It's due on Friday.
Parent Signature	**Teacher Signature**
I confirm that I have seen this rework plan and am available to lend a hand if it is needed.	I confirm that I have seen this rework plan and am available to lend a hand if it is needed.

Figure 3.1: Sample student rework plan for grade 8 science.

buildings (DuFour et al., 2016). The purpose of goal setting for both students and teachers is to reinforce the notion that growth is achieved through a recursive process of identifying needs and then taking tangible steps to address those needs. If we can teach students to make goal setting a regular part of their personal routine, we will also increase their commitment to assessing themselves.

We encourage teams to start by asking students to set and work toward achieving short-term goals. Here is why: If goal setting is going to become a part of the personal routine of students, they need to experience success early and often. "Goal setting," write Chappuis and Stiggins (2020), "is most satisfying when we see real progress toward the desired outcome. Part of the motivational hook for students and the key to re-engaging marginally interested students is tangible, hard evidence of progress" (p. 399). That means students are more likely to lean in when they are working toward short-term goals that they can master in a reasonable period than they are when working toward long-term goals.

Effective student goals (Chappuis & Stiggins, 2020) must include the following elements:

- A clear statement of the intended learning: "What do I need to learn?"

- A description of current status: "Where am I now with respect to my goal?"

- An action plan:

- "What steps will I take?"

- "When will I do this work?"

- "Where will I do this work?"

- "Who can I work with? What materials will I need?"

- "What will I use as my 'before' and 'after' pictures?" (pp. 395–396)

Can you see the parallels between this process and the process that collaborative teams use to develop SMART goals? Remember that the SMART goals collaborative teams develop (Conzemius & O'Neill, 2014) must be as follows.

- Strategic and specific
- Measurable
- Attainable
- Results oriented
- Time bound

Both frameworks require learners to use evidence to identify meaningful goals to pursue. Both frameworks also require learners to develop a plan for meeting their goals within a specific period. Those practices should be a part of any goal-setting work that you do with students.

For third-grade teacher Stephanie Van Horn, short-term goal setting is built around what she calls WOW—*working on weekly*—goals (Van Horn, 2014). Each week, students in Stephanie's classroom write on sticky notes to respond to the following two sentence starters (Van Horn, 2014).

- "In one week, I will _____."

- "I know I have made my goal when _____."

Using these sentence starters, students craft goals that sound like this.

- In one week, I will get to lesson five on Typing Pal. I know I have made my goal when I see a shiny red apple on lesson five.

- In one week, I will turn my homework in on time. I know I have made my goal because there will not be any assignments that say, "Late." (Van Horn, 2014)

Once students have completed their weekly WOW goals, they are posted by students on a chart at the back of the classroom. Students revisit their goals daily during their morning meetings. Doing so reminds learners that achieving goals takes regular monitoring and consistent effort over time. At the end of each week, Stephanie leads students in a reflection about their successes and their struggles. Then, students set new WOW goals for the following week (Van Horn, 2014).

By giving her students simple goal-setting sentence starters to complete, Stephanie has helped them to create goals that are strategic and specific, measurable, and time-bound—critical elements of any goal worth pursuing. And by encouraging students to focus on short-term goals, she has also ensured that the goals students set are immediately attainable, which is essential to convince learners to make goal setting a part of their academic routine. You can find a blank WOW goal-setting template to use with students on page 72.

To introduce older students to goal setting as a tool for self-assessment, consider having them create SMART goals (Conzemius & O'Neill, 2014) much like the ones collaborative teacher teams in PLCs develop. Because teachers working on learning teams in a PLC are already familiar with using SMART goals to develop action plans for their own growth, there should be little—if any—learning curve for using the same format with students. What is more, when teachers see the impact that SMART goals have on their students as learners, they are more likely to reinvest in the value of SMART goals as a tool for driving improvement on their collaborative teams.

The key to using SMART goals effectively with students is to develop processes for introducing SMART goals that are both age-appropriate and logical. Each term in the SMART acronym must be defined in student-friendly language—and students are going to need to see lots of examples of what strategic and specific, measurable, attainable, results-oriented, and

time-bound goals look like. Consider posting samples of goals for students and asking them to rate those samples for quality. Intentionally include samples that are not specific enough—or that are not attainable in a reasonable amount of time. Ask small groups to work together to revise those samples—and then to defend the reasoning behind their revisions. Doing so will build your students' capacity for goal setting—an essential first step for turning this work from an assignment that students must complete into a habit of mind. Figure 3.2 shows an example of this activity. See page 73 for a blank reproducible tool for using this activity with students.

	Student SMART Goal Examples	Evaluation Checklist
1	By the end of this semester, I want to set the school record for the mile run. That record is currently 6 minutes and 43 seconds. My current mile time is 8 minutes and 56 seconds. I am going to start running the mile run twice per week after school and time myself, so I have evidence of the progress that I am making.	**This SMART goal is:** ☐ Strategic and specific ☐ Measurable ☐ Attainable ☐ Results oriented ☐ Time bound
2	By the end of next week, I want to improve the score that I earned on my Major Events in the Revolutionary War exam. I earned a 63—but I think with review, I can raise that mark to an 80. What I need to review the most are all the laws that Britain passed that angered colonists. There were lots of questions about that—and I missed most of them.	**This SMART goal is:** ☐ Strategic and specific ☐ Measurable ☐ Attainable ☐ Results oriented ☐ Time bound
3	By the end of this school year, I want to be a better learner. That means I must work harder in all my classes. I am going to do that by paying attention and choosing the right friends. I should be able to see evidence that I am making progress in the grades that I am earning. I might even make it on the honor roll.	**This SMART goal is:** ☐ Strategic and specific ☐ Measurable ☐ Attainable ☐ Results oriented ☐ Time bound
4	I have always wanted to learn how to play the flute. To do that, I am going to sign up for band. My mother also told me that she would get me a private tutor if I proved to her that I was serious. I can do that by practicing at least 30 minutes a night after I get home from school. I think I can figure out how to play at least four songs without too much trouble.	**This SMART goal is:** ☐ Strategic and specific ☐ Measurable ☐ Attainable ☐ Results oriented ☐ Time bound

Sorting task: Now that you have evaluated each of the student SMART goal examples, work with a partner to use the following table to rank them in order from "In Need of the Most Revisions" to "Close to Perfect." Don't forget to defend your reasoning for each of your rankings.

Figure 3.2: SMART goal sorting activity.

continued →

	Rank-Ordered List of Examples	Reasoning for Our Rankings
The Student SMART Goal example **IN NEED OF THE MOST REVISIONS** is number:	SMART goal 3	This goal is too general. Things like "working hard and paying attention" aren't really specific actions that you can take. Also, this goal isn't very time bound because it gives the student the whole year to master it.
	SMART goal 4	This goal is getting a little more specific. The student mentions learning to play four songs on the flute as their goal—which is measurable—and practicing for thirty minutes a night—which is a specific step. This goal is missing a deadline.
	SMART goal 1	We think this goal is specific and measurable. The student knows exactly what he wants to accomplish and knows exactly where he is starting from. We just don't think this goal is attainable. You can't really improve your running time that much by practicing twice a week.
The Student SMART Goal example that is **CLOSE TO PERFECT** is number:	SMART goal 2	This goal is specific in a lot of ways. The student describes when he wants to take his retest. He also describes what he should study in order to raise his grade. We also like that this is a short-term goal because it means he is more likely to actually complete it.

Once your students understand each of the individual components of a SMART goal, they can create one for themselves. To scaffold this work, we suggest that you start by having students look carefully at an assessment or an assignment that they have just completed and that you would like them to rework. Ask your students, working independently or with a side partner, to identify elements of their products or performances that can be improved. Have them brainstorm steps that they could take to make those improvements. Push them to set a realistic deadline for completing the improvements, and then provide time during subsequent class periods for students to implement their plans. By focusing first on using goal setting to improve assignments that were recently completed and providing time for students to work through their action plan directly in class, you reinforce the notion that goal setting should lead to action that we can take today to produce results tomorrow.

On page 75 you will find a reproducible template "Developing a Student SMART Goal" that older students can use to write SMART goals.

Have Students Keep a Record of Their Progress

If students are going to become skilled at self-assessment, they are also going to need multiple opportunities to keep records of—and to report on—the progress that they are making (Chappuis, 2015; Chappuis & Stiggins, 2020). Regular record-keeping provides students with *evidence of their own ability*—a key to building confidence in every learner (Chappuis, 2015). And asking students to report on their progress serves as a powerful reminder that they really can move their *own* learning forward. "When students are prepared well over an extended period to tell the story of their own success (or lack thereof)," write assessment experts Stiggins and Chappuis (2005), "they experience a fundamental shift in their internal sense of responsibility for that success" (p. 3).

For author and middle school teacher Bill Ferriter, regular opportunities for students to keep records of the progress they are making are centered on a tool he calls a unit overview sheet (figure 3.3). Each unit overview sheet Bill develops with his collaborative team includes these elements.

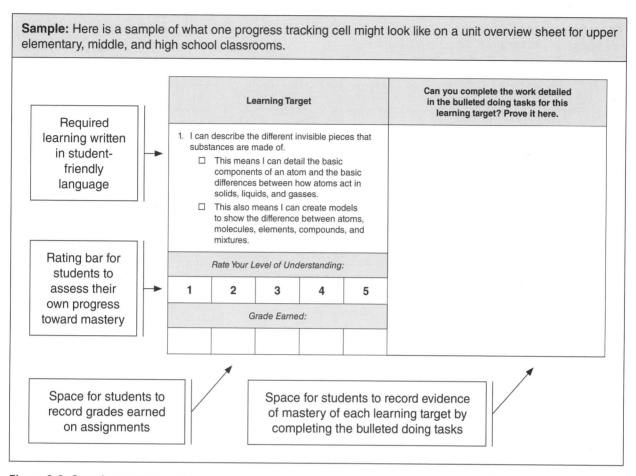

Figure 3.3: Sample progress tracking cell on a unit overview sheet for upper elementary, middle, and high school classrooms.

- A list of all the essential outcomes covered during a unit of study, written in student-friendly language

- Rating bars that allow students to regularly track changes over time in their level of mastery of each essential outcome

- Bulleted *doing tasks* that students can complete as demonstrations of mastery

- A list of all the vocabulary words covered during the unit of study

Students begin every cycle of instruction in Bill's classroom by reviewing their new unit overview sheet and giving themselves initial ratings for each essential outcome that represents their current levels of mastery. For most students, those initial ratings are ones or twos, providing evidence to students that they have a lot of learning to do.

Then, Bill asks his students to take out their unit overview sheets two or three times every week for regular progress checks. Sometimes, those progress checks

happen at the beginning of a lesson. "We are working on the first outcome on our unit overview sheet today," Bill will say. "Turn to a partner and share your current level of mastery. What do you know about this outcome already?" Other times, those checks happen at the end of a lesson. "We spent the last few days working on the second outcome on your unit overview sheet," Bill will say. "Do you know more now than you did when we started our lesson? If so, do you need to change your rating on your rating bar or add any evidence to the proof box on your unit overview sheet?"

Over the course of an entire cycle of instruction—which can last anywhere from three to six weeks—Bill's students will make dozens of changes to their unit overview sheets (see figure 3.4, page 64). Those changes include the following.

- Updating the rating bar for each essential outcome as they learn more

- Checking off the bullets for doing tasks that they have successfully completed

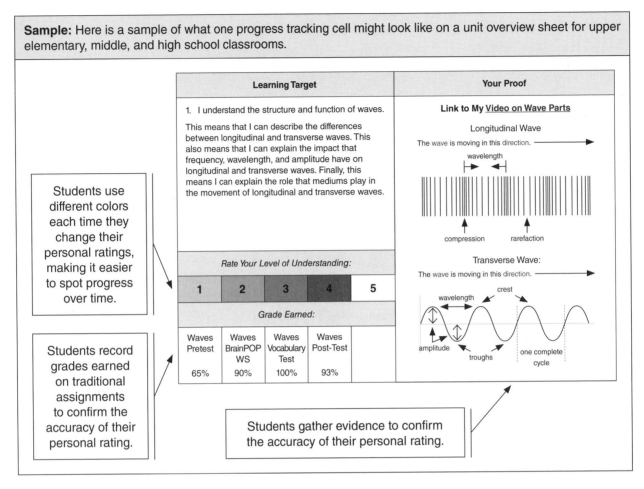

Figure 3.4: Sample progress tracking unit overview sheet showing student notes.

- Highlighting vocabulary words that they have mastered
- Adding grades that they earn on traditional assignments—quizzes, tests, worksheets, lab reports—which become evidence that confirms or challenges the accuracy of their personal ratings
- Filling proof boxes for each essential outcome with evidence—images or video that they take of classroom tasks, notes that they record during or after instruction, links to assignments completed that are stored in their Google Drives

Each time students return to their unit overview sheets in Bill's classroom, they can find evidence of both the learning they have already done and the learning they still must do. More important, each time students return to their unit overview sheets, they can find evidence that they really *are* learners.

Every doing task they complete, vocabulary word that they highlight, and rating that they change serves as tangible confirmation of their ability—an important factor for building a growth mindset in students (Dweck, 2016).

You can find a reproducible template for creating your own "Unit Overview Sheet" on page 77. Visit https://bit.ly/blankunitoverview to access a digital template for creating your own unit overview sheets.

Giving students regular opportunities to keep records of the progress they are making is also a priority for the faculty of Mason Crest Elementary School in northern Virginia. To make the process more approachable for primary learners, however, the teachers developed primary progress tracking cards for each essential outcome in their required curriculum (see figure 3.5).

In many ways, primary progress tracking cards work just like unit overview sheets. Each card includes an

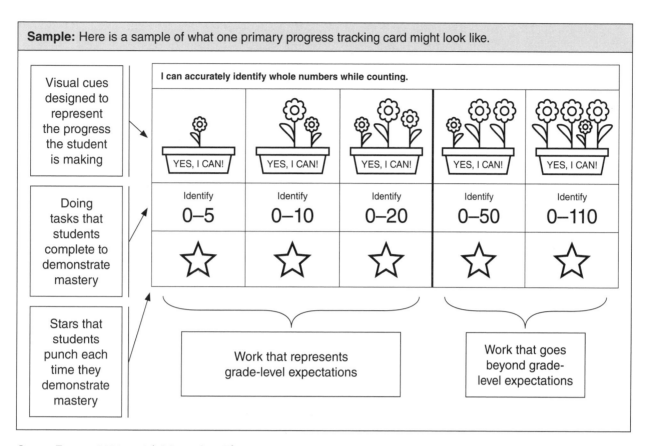

Sample: Here is a sample of what one primary progress tracking card might look like.

Visual cues designed to represent the progress the student is making

Doing tasks that students complete to demonstrate mastery

Stars that students punch each time they demonstrate mastery

I can accurately identify whole numbers while counting.

YES, I CAN!	YES, I CAN!	YES, I CAN!	YES, I CAN!	YES, I CAN!
Identify 0–5	Identify 0–10	Identify 0–20	Identify 0–50	Identify 0–110
☆	☆	☆	☆	☆

Work that represents grade-level expectations

Work that goes beyond grade-level expectations

Source: Ferriter, 2020, p. 94; Mason Crest Elementary, 2017.

Figure 3.5: Primary progress tracking card.

essential outcome written in student-friendly language. Each card also includes several doing tasks that students can complete to demonstrate mastery. Finally, each card provides students with a chance to track the progress they are making.

Teachers in primary classrooms at Mason Crest Elementary copy their progress tracking cards on card stock for each student. Each card measures approximately two inches wide by four inches long, making them easy for primary students to handle. Cards are bundled together with metal book rings to become a complete set that students carry with them from learning station to learning station. Students then use a star-shaped hole punch to mark off doing tasks they successfully complete at learning stations during a cycle of instruction. Over time, the bundled collection of hole-punched cards becomes a source of pride for primary students—proof that they are making progress as learners.

You can find a reproducible template "Primary Progress Tracking Card" on page 79. Visit http://bit.ly /primaryprogresstracking to access a digital template for creating primary progress tracking cards.

As Ute Prince, a kindergarten teacher in the Fremont Unified School District in California, learned more about the importance of student self-assessment from author Bill Ferriter during a professional development session, she knew it was something she wanted to integrate into her instruction (U. Prince, personal communication, October 15, 2017). But she also knew she did not want to create primary progress tracking cards because she thought they would be difficult for young students to keep up with over time. Together with Bill, she brainstormed a paper-free strategy for integrating self-assessment into the work that she was doing with her students.

Lessons would start as they always did in Ute's classroom, in a circle on the classroom carpet. She would introduce students to the goal for the week and ask them to share what they already knew about the learning they were about to begin. After that conversation ended, Ute's plan was to ask students to place a magnetic foam animal on a five-point grid on her classroom whiteboard as a representation of their current level of mastery with the essential outcome they would be working on (figure 3.6). Ute would then take a picture of those initial ratings to capture evidence of where her class thought they were as learners before learning even began.

At the end of each week, Ute planned to bring her students back to the carpet for another conversation about their learning. Much like the informal conversations that Bill structured around unit overview sheets, Ute planned to ask students to share evidence that they had made progress toward mastering the outcome of the week. Finally, she would ask her students whether they needed to move their foam farm animal forward on the classroom learning grid. Each student would return to his or her original foam farm animal and move it to the spot on the grid that best represented his or her new level of mastery. (See figure 3.7.)

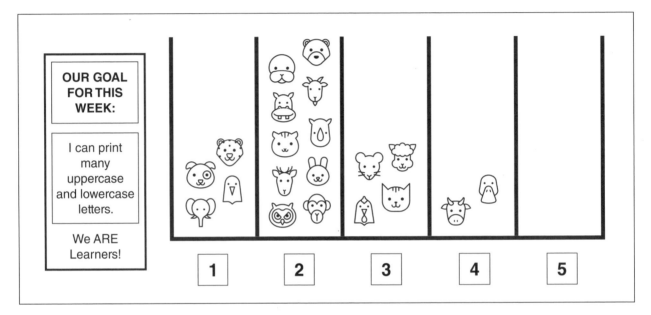

Source: Adapted from Ute Prince, 2017, Fremont Unified School District.

Figure 3.6: Paper-free strategy for self-assessment.

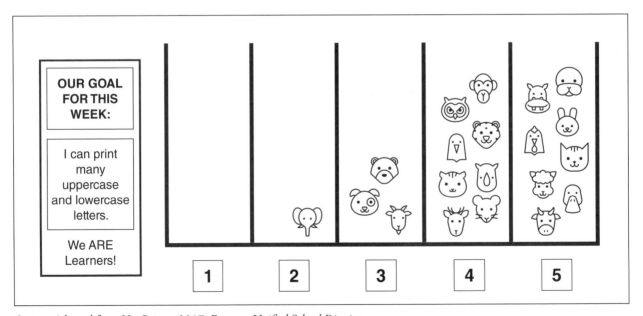

Source: Adapted from Ute Prince, 2017, Fremont Unified School District.

Figure 3.7: Paper-free strategy for self-assessment at end of week.

As this conversation with her students ended, Ute planned to share the before learning picture that she had taken at the beginning of the week. Doing so would prove to her students that they were a classroom full of learners because their foam farm animals were moving forward after a week of instruction.

The key takeaway in each of these examples is that there is no *one right format* for integrating progress tracking or record keeping into your work with students. In fact, the teachers in each of the examples would tell you that the format they chose is simply a tool for giving students lots of opportunities to reflect on the trajectory of their own learning, and that it is those opportunities for self-reflection that matter most. Your goal, then, should be to identify a process for integrating progress tracking and record keeping into your classroom practice that you believe in and then make that work a part of your everyday instruction.

Recommendations for Getting Started

Few people know more about the reasons that high school students drop out than author and researcher Deborah Feldman. Together with her colleagues Anthony Smith and Barbara Waxman, Feldman interviewed fifty high school dropouts while writing *"Why We Drop Out": Understanding and Disrupting Student Pathways to Leaving School* (Feldman et al., 2017). In an interview with Cindy Long (2017) of *NEA Today* magazine, Feldman explains that academic challenge starting years earlier is often the original impetus for high school students deciding to leave school for good:

> There were very distinct patterns we see with kids starting to pull away usually in middle school. The through line in many of their stories was some kind of academic challenge that undermined their faith in themselves as learners, that then led to helplessness and hopelessness about their ability to be a student, which was their primary job in life.

Think about that for a moment. Imagine how difficult it must be for students to continue to persevere in school once they begin to doubt their own ability to succeed academically. No wonder so many give up.

How do we keep students from doubting their own ability as learners? Our argument is simple, keeping students from doubting their own ability as learners depends on turning students into capable partners in the assessment process. Doing so ensures that classrooms become feedback-rich environments where students learn to accurately identify gaps in their mastery and take steps to address those gaps. Here are a few recommendations to help you create that kind of feedback-rich environment in your classroom: (1) avoid giving grades for as long as possible, (2) don't be surprised when students are not truthful, and (3) trust yourself.

Avoid Giving Grades for as Long as Possible

Many teachers believe in grading as a tool to both motivate and evaluate learner performance. If you look carefully at the research, grades *can* motivate learners—*if* learners feel like the goals they are working toward are within their grasp and see grades as feedback about their progress toward mastery instead of as a reflection of their ability (Guskey, 2019; Wiliam, 2012). When learners feel like they cannot compete, however, they simply give up (Wiliam, 2012). This explains why so many struggling students lose faith in themselves. Earn one too many poor marks, and you become convinced that it is impossible to compete against both the goals set by your instructors and the students sitting next to you in the classroom. It also explains why top-performing students avoid the most challenging goals. Slipping into a performance orientation toward learning, earning high marks on easy tasks becomes more important to successful students than risking earning low marks on more difficult work (Wiliam, 2012).

What is the solution? Borrow a strategy from Leah Alcala (n.d.)—the middle school mathematics teacher spotlighted in the previous section—and avoid giving grades for as long as you can. Remember that for students in traditional schools, grades signify that learning has ended. Also remember that students easily misinterpret the meaning behind the scores they have earned. When asked, "How did you do on the test?" students most often report their score and define their effort solely by that score—"Terrible. I earned a 65 percent." That surface-level interpretation of mastery *or* of failure shows just how important it is for teachers to orchestrate a student's deeper dive into his or her marks to discover strengths and weaknesses as well as to set goals for continued improvement. All that work is lost as soon as you put grades on papers or scores in your gradebook.

Don't Be Surprised When Students Are Not Truthful

The most common question audiences ask when we speak about the role that student self-assessment can play in classrooms is always, "Do your students ever tell you that they have mastered an outcome when you know that they haven't?" Our answer always catches audiences off guard, "Yep. Happens all the time. Especially early in the school year." Think about that for a moment. Why would students not be truthful about their assessment of their own performance early in the school year? More important, why would teachers continue a practice knowing that students are not telling the truth about their own performance?

Students are not truthful about their performance early in the school year because they have already learned that struggling in school brings unwanted consequences. Earn a poor mark? Your teacher is going to call home, and your parents are going to take away your favorite hobby and make you go to a tutor instead. Struggle on an important assignment? You are going to miss recess to rework the task. Bomb an end-of-grade exam? You are going to lose one of your elective periods and spend that time instead in a remediation class with a teacher. The result of these consequences of struggling is that students learn that it is easier to disguise their weaknesses and pretend like they are succeeding even when they are not (Brown, 2020).

Disrupting this pattern of behavior starts by reminding students again and again that their self-assessments are never going to end up in your gradebook. Instead, their self-assessments are designed to give them information that they can use to improve their own performance. Point out that you do not need their self-assessments to rate their progress. You are still giving and scoring traditional assignments. Encourage students to see honest self-assessment as a tool for identifying concepts that they have mastered and concepts that they are still working to master. "Telling the truth when you assess yourself," you can say, "gives you information on the steps that you can take to get better at learning the things that you are expected to learn this year."

Your students will not believe you at first. They are too conditioned by years of schooling to think that a teacher would spend time on something in class that is not going to be scored. But over time, they will realize that you were telling the truth all along. And at that point, self-assessment will move from a "practice my teacher uses to generate grades" in the minds of students to "a practice my teacher uses to help me to know how I am doing at mastering important stuff."

Trust Yourself

Whenever we ask teachers to explain the gap between what they believe about student self-assessment ("It's incredibly important!") and how often they integrate opportunities for student self-assessment into their instruction ("Not very often"), we hear one answer repeatedly: "We know that self-assessment matters, but we just don't have the time to integrate it into our instruction."

That answer makes sense, doesn't it? After all, preparing students to be capable partners in the assessment process does take a lot of time. First, we must convince students that assessment *is* their responsibility. That simple notion runs contrary to the traditional patterns in schools, where teachers complete assessment, not students. Then, we need to teach students to look carefully at their work to find evidence of how they are doing. That can be a complex and time-consuming process as well. Students will not automatically know what success looks like—or be able to accurately rate how close they are toward meeting expectations—without regular opportunities to practice the skills of self-assessment. Given that teachers and schools are held accountable for teaching massive curricula (Marzano, 2017) and for ensuring that students meet growth targets on high-stakes standardized tests, making time for student self-assessment can feel like a professional risk.

In the moments when you begin to doubt the value of student self-assessment, trust yourself. Remember that Hattie's (2017) research shows that there is nothing that we can do in our classrooms that has a higher probability of considerably accelerating student achievement than making student self-assessment a regular part of our instruction. As Grant Wiggins (2012) explains:

> Although the universal teacher lament that there's no time for feedback is understandable, remember that "no time to give and use feedback" actually means "no time to cause learning." As we have seen, research shows that less teaching plus more feedback is the key to achieving greater learning.

Now, a word to principals: If school leaders want teachers to make student self-assessment a regular part of the work that they do in their classrooms—*and they should*—they need to be vocal about their support for the practice. To make time for student self-assessment, teams may need to teach less of their required curriculum. Leaders should let them know that they support that professional decision. If teams are using evidence of performance to identify small handfuls of essential outcomes unit-by-unit that every student must master— and then taking responsible steps to intervene when students need interventions or extensions—it is OK to prioritize self-assessment over coverage of curricula. Doing so will both encourage and empower students, and in the end, our goal as educators should be to leave every student encouraged and empowered.

Concluding Thoughts

In *Learning by Doing: A Handbook for Professional Learning Communities at Work*, DuFour and his colleagues (2016) define a PLC as:

> An ongoing process in which educators work collaboratively in recurring cycles of collective inquiry and action research to achieve better results for the students they serve. PLCs operate under the assumption that the key to improved learning for students is continuous, job-embedded learning for educators. (p. 10)

The goal of collaborative teams in a PLC, then, is to use collective inquiry and action research to build shared knowledge about their practice together. That shared knowledge develops as teachers experiment with and document the impact of varied strategies and then set aside time to share their successes, failures, and modifications with one another.

Given the well-documented impact that high-quality formative assessment practices can have on achievement, we cannot think of anything that is *more* important for collaborative teams to study together than the way that they use assessment to improve learning. Need proof? Then consider that Dylan Wiliam and Paul Black—two of the foremost experts on assessment in schools—determined that "attention to the use of assessment to inform instruction, particularly at the classroom level, in many cases effectively doubled the speed of learning" (Wiliam, 2011, p. 36). Imagine the immediate difference that educators could make in the success of every learner if collaborative teams committed themselves to increasing their shared expertise in the principles and theories of assessment for learning.

It is important to remember, however, that collaborative teams miss an opportunity when they focus only on using assessments *to inform their instruction*. Instead, our collective work should also focus on developing strategies to encourage students *to take ownership over their own learning*. The all-too-common cycle in schools—where students make quick judgments about their likelihood of success before deciding to invest in the work that we are asking them to do— needs to be interrupted by carefully designed efforts to integrate student self-assessment into classrooms. As Organisation for Economic Co-operation and Development (OECD, 2008) researchers explain:

> Ultimately, the goal of formative assessment is to guide students toward the development of their own "learning to learn" skills (also sometimes referred to as "metacognitive" strategies). Students are thus equipped with their own language and tools for learning and are more likely to transfer and apply these skills for problem solving into daily life; they strengthen their ability to find answers or develop strategies for addressing problems with which they are not familiar. In other words, they develop strong "control" strategies for their own learning.

Odds are that your collaborative team has already embraced common formative assessment as a tool for studying your instruction and for tracking progress by both student and standard. You have probably developed assessments that you believe in and that are carefully aligned to the outcomes that you have identified as essential. You probably also have tools that you use to learn from—and act on—the assessment data you are collecting. This shared work is meaningful and important, but it remains incomplete until your team works together to figure out how to use self-assessment to better equip your students with the language and tools for learning.

Student Rework Plan

Student Name: _____

Directions: To raise your score on your recent test or project, you must use this template to develop and then complete a rework plan. When you have completed your rework plan, please have it signed by both your teacher and your parents.

Name of Assignment You Are Reworking:	
Questions to Consider	**Your Response**
What did you struggle with on your initial attempt at this assignment? Were there things that you did not know? Things that you were not sure how to do? Did you make any of the common mistakes that we reviewed in class? Which ones?	
What steps will you take to correct the mistakes that you made on your initial attempt at this assignment? Are there concepts that you need to review again? Do you need some extra practice problems? Will you attend a review session or find a classmate to lend a hand?	
Where will you turn if you need help? What resources are available to you to help you correct your mistakes? Is your teacher offering a rework session? Do you have a classmate that can lend a hand? Are there resources like textbooks or handouts that can help?	
When will your rework be finished?	
Parent Signature:	**Teacher Signature:**
I confirm that I have seen this rework plan and am available to lend a hand if it is needed.	I confirm that I have seen this rework plan and am available to lend a hand if it is needed.

WOW Goals

For third-grade teacher Stephanie Van Horn (2014), short-term goal setting starts by asking students to complete two sentence starters on sticky notes to create what she calls WOW—*working on weekly*—goals. Once students have completed their WOW goals, they add their sticky notes to a chart in the back of the classroom and revisit during daily morning meetings. You can replicate this work in your own classroom by making copies of the following WOW goal templates and asking students to fill one out at the beginning of every week.

MY WOW GOAL:

In one week, I will:

I will know that I have made my goal when:

MY WOW GOAL:

In one week, I will:

I will know that I have made my goal when:

MY WOW GOAL:

In one week, I will:

I will know that I have made my goal when:

MY WOW GOAL:

In one week, I will:

I will know that I have made my goal when:

Source: Van Horn, S. (2014, November 7). Working on weekly class SMART goals [Blog post]. Accessed at www.3rdgradethoughts.com/2014/11/working-on-weekly-class-smart-goals.html on June 28, 2020.

Rating and Ranking Student SMART Goals

Student Name: _____

Directions: Read the four examples of student SMART goals below. Then, work with a partner to determine whether each example includes all the elements of a good SMART goal. As a reminder, SMART goals should be:

STRATEGIC AND SPECIFIC	MEASURABLE	ATTAINABLE	RESULTS ORIENTED	TIME BOUND
Answers the question, *"What do I want to accomplish?"*	Answers the question, *"How will I know when I have achieved this goal?"*	Answers the question, *"Is this goal realistic for me to try to accomplish?"*	Answers the question, *"What evidence can I collect to prove that I have accomplished this goal?"*	Answers the question, *"When do I want to have this goal completed by?"*

	Student SMART Goal Examples	Evaluation Checklist
1	By the end of this semester, I want to set the school record for the mile run. That record is currently 6 minutes and 43 seconds. My current mile time is 8 minutes and 56 seconds. I am going to start running the mile run twice per week after school and time myself, so I have evidence of the progress that I am making.	**This SMART goal is:** ☐ Strategic and specific ☐ Measurable ☐ Attainable ☐ Results oriented ☐ Time bound
2	By the end of next week, I want to improve the score that I earned on my Major Events in the Revolutionary War exam. I earned a 63—but I think with review, I can raise that mark to an 80. What I need to review the most are all the laws that Britain passed that angered colonists. There were lots of questions about that—and I missed most of them.	**This SMART goal is:** ☐ Strategic and specific ☐ Measurable ☐ Attainable ☐ Results oriented ☐ Time bound
3	By the end of this school year, I want to be a better learner. That means I must work harder in all my classes. I am going to do that by paying attention and choosing the right friends. I should be able to see evidence that I am making progress in the grades that I am earning. I might even make it on the honor roll.	**This SMART goal is:** ☐ Strategic and specific ☐ Measurable ☐ Attainable ☐ Results oriented ☐ Time bound
4	I have always wanted to learn how to play the flute. To do that, I am going to sign up for band. My mother also told me that she would get me a private tutor if I proved to her that I was serious. I can do that by practicing at least 30 minutes a night after I get home from school. I think I can figure out how to play at least four songs without too much trouble.	**This SMART goal is:** ☐ Strategic and specific ☐ Measurable ☐ Attainable ☐ Results oriented ☐ Time bound

Sorting Task: Now that you have evaluated each of the student SMART goal examples, work with a partner to use the following table to rank them in order from "In Need of the MOST Revisions" to "Close to Perfect." Don't forget to defend your reasoning for each of your rankings.

page 1 of 2

	RANK-ORDERED LIST OF EXAMPLES:	REASONING FOR OUR RANKINGS:
The Student SMART Goal example **IN NEED OF THE MOST REVISIONS** is number:		
The Student SMART Goal example that is **CLOSE TO PERFECT** is number:		

page 2 of 2

Developing a Student SMART Goal

Directions: Complete the following template to develop a SMART goal to guide your work in class over the next few weeks.

Name:
Date:
Your Goal:

Is your goal . . .				
STRATEGIC AND SPECIFIC Answers the question, *"What do I want to accomplish?"*	**MEASURABLE** Answers the question, *"How will I know when I have achieved this goal?"*	**ATTAINABLE** Answers the question, *"Is this goal realistic for me to try to accomplish?"*	**RESULTS ORIENTED** Answers the question, *"What evidence can I collect to prove that I have accomplished this goal?"*	**TIME BOUND** Answers the question, *"When do I want to have this goal completed by?"*

Obstacles and Setbacks

What are the obstacles that you can foresee getting in the way of accomplishing your goal? What are some solutions or actions that you can take to overcome these obstacles and potential setbacks?

Obstacles	Solutions or Actions

page 1 of 2

Action Items and Tasks

List at least five action items or tasks to help you achieve your goal. Assign target dates for completing each action item or task. Record when you have completed each action item or task.

Action Item or Task	Target Date	Completed Date

Reflection

Once you have completed this SMART goal, answer the following reflection questions.

Question	Your Response
What went well while you were working to accomplish this SMART goal? *Did you use any learning strategies that were particularly effective? Were there any resources that you used that helped you to move your learning forward?*	
What could have gone better while you were working to accomplish this SMART goal? *Was there anything about your SMART goal that needed to be revised while you were working? Were some obstacles hard for you to overcome? Why? What would you do differently the next time that you are working to accomplish a SMART goal?*	

Unit Overview Sheet

Unit:

Essential Questions:

❑	❑	❑
❑	❑	❑

Learning Target	Your Proof

Rate Your Level of Understanding				
1	2	3	4	5

Grades Earned				

Learning Target	Your Proof

Rate Your Level of Understanding				
1	2	3	4	5

Grades Earned				

page 1 of 2

Learning Target	Your Proof

Rate Your Level of Understanding				
1	2	3	4	5

Grades Earned				

Learning Target	Your Proof

Rate Your Level of Understanding				
1	2	3	4	5

Grades Earned				

Vocabulary to Master				
❑	❑	❑	❑	❑
❑	❑	❑	❑	❑
❑	❑	❑	❑	❑
❑	❑	❑	❑	❑
❑	❑	❑	❑	❑

Primary Progress Tracking Card

Here is a blank template that you can use to create your own primary progress tracking card.

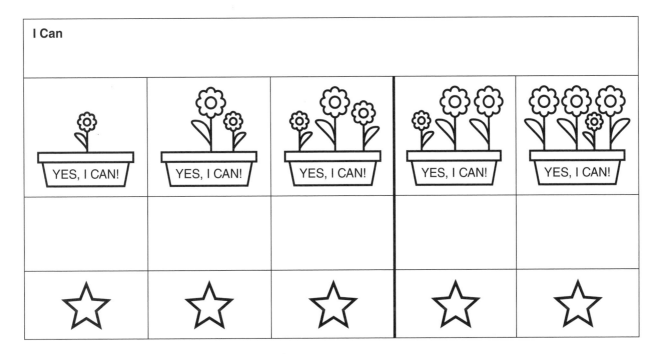

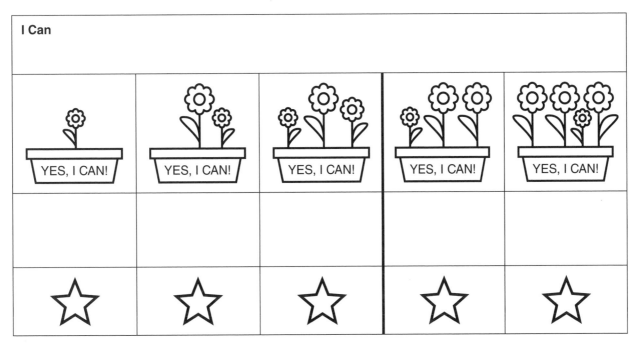

Source: Adapted from Mason Crest Elementary School, 2017. Used with permission.

4 Helping Students Take Action

The fourth-grade teachers at Elmhurst Elementary School worked together on a high-functioning collaborative team. They had been receiving support and coaching on the PLC at Work process for two years. They enjoyed working together and had reached the stage where they were writing common formative assessments, sharing data, discussing instructional strategies that worked, and identifying students in need of additional time and support for learning. Every member of the team cared about their students and wanted to do the absolute best on their behalf.

As part of the coaching experience, the team opened their classrooms for observations to receive feedback on their instruction. They were invested in this process because they had a desire to see more students succeeding in their high-poverty school. James Samuelson, the newest member of the team and a first-year teacher, was especially interested in growing in his knowledge and skills since he had not taken the traditional steps to becoming a teacher. Having just made the switch from a career in sales to a career in the classroom, he was working on a provisional certification and excited for the opportunity to receive feedback from the instructional coach who was mentoring him.

One day, James was passing back science tests to his students. His instructional coach happened to be standing next to a group of six boys. As they received their papers, each boy saw immediately how he had done on the test. Within their table group, one boy had scored a perfect ten out of ten. The other members of the group had failed the test. None had scored higher than a five out of ten. James told the students not to worry about their scores because he would be going over the test in just a moment. First, however, he wanted students to know how the scores looked for the entire class. "We had two students with a 10/10, two students with a 9/10, three students with an 8/10, and everyone else had a 5/10 or less," he announced.

The coach, out of the corner of her eye, noticed that as James was announcing how the class had done on the test, the five boys who had failed at the table group she was standing next to were smiling and high-fiving each other. She thought, "Wow! They are celebrating their failure." She also noticed that the one boy in the group who had passed with a perfect score had quickly put his test away so that the other boys in his group would not know how he had done.

Think about that for a moment. Why would students celebrate their failure on a classroom test? The answer is connected to thoughts that we explored in the previous chapter. For many students, the grades they earn on an assessment can be easily misinterpreted as an endpoint in a cycle of instruction and as an indication of personal ability. The high-fiving students were certainly not proud of their scores. They did not set out to fail the test. After all, no student *wants* to fail. Their reaction is a defense mechanism in an exceedingly difficult and embarrassing moment, and a way of feeling good through commonality of experience when they were not able to feel good about their learning experience.

What is interesting about this reaction is that collaborative teams in PLCs *do not* see grades earned on assessments or assignments as an end point in a cycle of instruction. Instead, collaborative teams in PLCs see grades earned on assessments or assignments as *an invitation to action* at the midpoint of a cycle of instruction. Teams use assessment results to plan their responses to the third and fourth critical questions of a PLC (DuFour et al., 2016): How will we respond when students do not learn? and, How will we respond to students who are already proficient? Grades, then, are not an *indication of a student's ability* to the teachers on collaborative teams. They are an *indication of a student's current level of mastery*—useful tools for guiding next professional steps.

The mistake that many collaborative teams in PLCs make is forgetting that grades earned on assessments or assignments are not just an invitation for *teachers to act*. When teams are open to exploring different learner-centered approaches for responding to assessment evidence, grades earned can become an invitation for *students to act* as well. Our goal should be to provide students with the know-how to answer two student-centered variations of the third and fourth critical questions of learning: What steps should I take when I am struggling to master important outcomes? and How can I extend my learning after I have mastered important outcomes? This chapter will show you how to begin doing that work in your classroom.

Why Is This Important to Learners?

Before the benefits of using assessment as a tool for guiding next actions became widely understood in education, most teachers followed the process James used when giving an exam. A teacher would administer a test after the class spent a few days completing study guides or playing review games. The teacher would then grade the test within a reasonable amount of time. After grading the tests, the teacher would record scores in his or her gradebook, pass papers back to the class, and then go over the test for the next thirty to forty-five minutes. Rarely did teachers reflect on—or ask questions about the efficacy of—this practice.

Unfortunately, this process—which continues in many classrooms—often has a negative impact on a student's desire to succeed in school. Regardless of the intention of teachers, grades—which "channel students' attention to the self and away from the task" (Lipnevich & Smith, 2008, p. 6)—reinforce a student's narrative about his or her intellectual capacity and academic reputation with peers (Bandura, 1997). "Students who

come well-prepared cognitively and motivationally learn quickly and are adequately served by the prevailing educational practices" (p. 175), writes Albert Bandura (1997), an expert on developing self-efficacy in learners. Traditional grading practices that result in social competition, however, "convert educational experiences into ones where many are doomed to failure for the high success of a few" (Bandura, 1997, p. 175).

Bandura's work on self-efficacy is highly instructive for teachers who are interested in helping students develop the skills necessary to act after collecting evidence on their current levels of mastery. To Bandura (2009), self-efficacy is the belief that a person can positively influence both the events and outcomes that they face in their lives. People with a high sense of self-efficacy see difficult tasks as challenges to be mastered. On the other hand, people with a low sense of self-efficacy are likely to give up when circumstances get challenging. As Bandura (2009) explains, "Unless people believe that they can produce desired effects and forestall undesired ones by their actions, they have little incentive to act or to persevere in the face of difficulties" (Location No. 4919). More important, people with a high sense of self-efficacy see struggle as a function of *skills that they have yet to master* instead of *ability that they will never have* (Bandura, 2009).

Bandura (2009) argues that our sense of self-efficacy develops in response to four primary influences.

1. **Mastery experiences:** Nothing has a greater impact on our sense of self-efficacy than experiencing success in mastering challenging goals through "perseverant effort" (Location No. 5052). Each successful mastery experience earned through "resilient efficacy" (Location No. 5052) leaves us convinced that we have what it takes to tackle new challenges in the future. Easy successes with quick results, however, can cause us to question our own abilities when we struggle—particularly for people who do not already have a well-established sense of self-efficacy.

2. **Vicarious experiences:** For Bandura, vicarious experiences refer to the impact that social role models can have on the development of self-efficacy in people. Seeing others succeed at tackling challenging tasks leaves us convinced that we can succeed at

the same tasks. "Competent models," writes Bandura (2009), "convey knowledge, skills and strategies for managing task demands" (Location No. 5052). Vicarious experiences are only meaningful, however, when social models remind us of ourselves. The success or struggles of models whom we perceive to be significantly different from us do little to influence our own sense of efficacy.

3. **Social persuasion:** Sometimes, convincing people that they can succeed in the face of challenge depends on nothing more than some well-timed words of encouragement. "If people are persuaded to believe in themselves," explains Bandura (2009), "they will exert more effort" (Location No. 5052). Efforts to increase efficacy through social persuasion, however, must be realistic. Encouraging people to tackle challenging tasks only to see them fail in those efforts can have a negative impact on self-efficacy.

4. **Emotional and physiological states:** Finally, our confidence in our own abilities to tackle challenging tasks is influenced by our response to stressful situations. For some, stressful situations are a motivator, heightening determination to persist in the face of difficulty. Others "read their tension, anxiety and weariness as signs of personal deficiencies" (Bandura, 2009, Location No. 5077). Similarly, a positive attitude toward challenge increases efficacy while a negative attitude toward challenge decreases efficacy (Bandura, 2009).

Think back to the students who failed James's test in the story that started this chapter. Their response to failure—full of high-fives and laughter—is evidence of students who have a low sense of self-efficacy. And unfortunately, James's instructional choices reinforced the doubts that his students already have about themselves as learners. Not only did they fail in the face of a challenging task, they were surrounded by social role models—peers both at their table and in their classroom—who also earned poor marks. What is more, their teacher's encouragement—"Don't worry about your scores because we are going over answers in a moment"—likely rang hollow to students who got more than half of the questions wrong on the test.

As a result, James's students are left with no reason to believe they can be successful in his science class. "It is difficult to achieve much," Bandura (1995) argues, "while fighting self-doubt" (p. 6).

So, how do teachers create learning spaces that build the intellectual efficacy of struggling students? For Bandura (1994), the first step is to emphasize self-comparisons over social comparisons in classrooms. Teachers should make every effort to ensure all learners can "expand their competencies" (p. 12), seeing not only the individual progress they are making, but next steps that are worth taking. Well-structured cooperative activities can also build self-efficacy in struggling students. When cooperative activities are successful, struggling students "judge themselves more capable" (Bandura, 1997, p. 175) than when working on the same tasks alone. There is risk involved in using cooperative activities to build self-efficacy in struggling students, however. If those activities are a failure, all members of the unsuccessful group—high achievers *and* those who struggle—tend to "think less well of" (Bandura, 1997, p. 175) the students who came to the group with poor academic reputations to begin with.

For researchers Hattie and Clarke (2019), building intellectual efficacy depends on first acknowledging that feedback in schools—including in the form of grades—has traditionally been given to learners for a variety of purposes. We give feedback to reinforce success or to correct errors. We also give feedback to suggest improvements. Finally, we give feedback to reward or punish students (Hattie & Clarke, 2019). Some of those purposes—using feedback to reinforce success or suggest improvements—can have a positive impact on intellectual efficacy because they cause learners *to question their response to the task*. Others—using feedback to reward or punish—can have a negative impact on intellectual efficacy because they cause learners *to question themselves* (Hattie & Clarke, 2019). In the end, Hattie and Clarke (2019) argue that building intellectual efficacy depends less on providing students with lots of feedback and more on teaching students to "receive, interpret and use the feedback provided" (p. 5) to improve their own performance.

The distinction between students *questioning themselves* and *questioning their response to a task* is one that Nancy Frey, John Hattie, and Douglas Fisher (2018) explore in *Developing Assessment-Capable Visible Learners*.

Productive self-questioning happens when students reflect on what they know and think through next steps worth taking to move their own learning forward (Frey et al., 2018). Developing the skills to ask insightful questions about both progress and mastery does not have a positive impact just on a student's sense of self-efficacy, however. With an effect size of 0.64, developing the skills to ask insightful questions about both progress and mastery has a positive impact on a student's academic achievement (Hattie, 2012). As Frey and colleagues (2018) note:

> There's great value in self-questioning, as it can be a catalyst needed for monitoring one's own learning and making adjustments accordingly. The more we can move students to active decision making about their own learning, the more assessment capable they become. (p. 126)

There is a common thread running through this research. Self-efficacy is about something more than helping students feel good about who they are as learners. As positive psychology researcher Courtney Ackerman (2020) explains, "While self-esteem is focused more on 'being' (e.g., feeling that you are perfectly acceptable as you are), self-efficacy is more focused on 'doing' (e.g., feeling that you are up to a challenge)." Students with a high sense of self-efficacy are the perfect partners for teachers working in collaborative teams because they believe in their own ability to improve through action.

What Can This Look Like in Your Classroom?

Think for a moment about all the different ways that teachers give students feedback on their learning. They grade papers, filling them with detailed comments designed to draw student attention to places where their work could be improved; they respond to questions, addressing misconceptions in thinking; they track the progress students are making standard by standard through the curricula, sharing the patterns with both parents and students in regularly scheduled conferences or informal conversations that happen during class. The ongoing evaluation of performance is such an important part of the work of educators

that it would be difficult to count the number of times that a classroom teacher provides feedback to students during a regular school day.

It is important to remember, however, that the *amount of feedback* teachers give to learners has little to do with how *useful that feedback is* in attempts to develop students ready to take next steps on their own (Hattie & Clarke, 2019). If teachers are committed to helping learners find answers to the student-centered versions of the third and fourth critical questions in a PLC that we outline in the introduction of this chapter—"What steps should I take when I am struggling to master important outcomes?" and "How can I extend my learning after I have mastered important outcomes?"—we need to rethink the kind of feedback we are providing to students, remembering that the most meaningful feedback is focused on "changing the student rather than changing the work" (Wiliam, 2016).

The good news is that designing feedback experiences that change the student rather than changing the work is not that hard to do. Here are a few strategies worth exploring: (1) have students reflect on practice attempts before final demonstrations of mastery, (2) introduce students to logical next steps to move learning forward, (3) develop extension menus for each unit of study, and (4) help older students (typically beginning in grade 3) put grades in context.

Have Students Reflect on Practice Attempts Before Final Demonstrations of Mastery

One of the fundamental mistakes that James from the story that started this chapter made was giving his students a test that they were clearly not yet prepared to take. How do we know that his students were not yet prepared? Because more than half of his students earned a failing grade. If teachers in a PLC are using common formative assessment to adjust their instruction *during* a cycle of inquiry, there should never be a time when more than half of the students in a classroom fail an end-of-unit exam. Teachers on collaborative teams who recognize that many of their students are struggling to master the content covered during a unit of study would have provided additional lessons before asking students to complete such an important assessment.

The choice to move forward with his end-of-unit exam before his students were prepared for it will have *negative instructional implications* for James and his learning team. He will have to spend time reteaching students before he can begin his next unit. He will also have to provide extension opportunities for students who have already demonstrated mastery of the content. Both of those actions are likely to impact the pacing of his collaborative team. It is difficult to study and practice together, after all, when teachers are not in roughly the same place in their curriculum at roughly the same time.

The choice to move forward with his end-of-unit exam before his students were prepared for it also has *negative efficacy implications* for learners. Remember that experiencing success in mastering challenging goals is one of the most important ways to build the confidence that learners have in their own ability to improve and that experiencing failure leaves learners—particularly those with a low sense of self-efficacy to begin with—doubting themselves (Bandura, 2009; Chappuis & Stiggins, 2020). How could James have made this learning experience more positive for his students? He should have structured his instruction and assessment plans in a way that would have ensured success for more learners, rather than placing his students in a situation where they were all too likely to fail. As Bandura (2009) explains, "Effective efficacy builders do more than convey faith in others. They arrange situations for others in ways that bring success" (Location No. 5077).

If we were coaching James, we would recommend that he create structured opportunities for students to use a practice test in the week before the final exam as a tool *to reflect on where they currently are* in their attempts to master the key learnings from the unit and *to plan next steps* that they could take to better prepare for the final exam. Those are, after all, foundational behaviors of self-efficacious individuals.

What can using a practice test as a tool for reflection look like? The first step is to ask students to think about their current levels of mastery with key learnings covered in the unit before they are even introduced to the practice test. Teachers can accomplish this by listing the key learnings in approachable language and then asking students to respond to a series of prompts designed to promote reflection. Here is a sample from a fifth-grade fractions unit (figure 4.1, page 86).

Next, teachers could ask students to use a tracking template while taking and reviewing their practice test

(Chappuis, 2015; Chappuis & Stiggins, 2020). Here is a sample from the same fifth-grade fractions unit (figure 4.2, page 87).

Notice that this tracking template ties each question on the practice test to one of the key learnings from the unit. That is an essential first step to helping students to spot places where they are succeeding and places where they are struggling. Taking action depends on first gathering information—and for students, the most important information to gather is connected to the specific outcomes that they have already mastered and the outcomes that they are still working to master. Also notice that as students are reviewing their results on the practice test, they are asked to think through the reasons why they missed individual questions. Doing so will help them figure out the *right next steps* to take when preparing for their final exam. The actions necessary to correct errors made because of simple mistakes or misreading questions are different than the actions necessary to correct errors made because of deeper conceptual misunderstandings (Chappuis, 2015; Chappuis & Stiggins, 2020; Fisher & Frey, 2012).

Finally, after giving a practice test, teachers could ask students to use the information that they have gathered on their tracking templates to design a plan for preparing for the actual end-of-unit exam. Here is a sample from the fifth-grade fractions unit (figure 4.3, page 88).

Notice that the reflection questions on this planning template are designed to do more than point out to students the mistakes they made on the practice test. The reflection questions on this planning template are designed to prove to students that they *can* accurately assess the progress that they are making, to help students spot areas where they *have been* successful as learners, and to encourage students to take targeted next steps toward turning their end-of-unit exam into a *positive mastery experience* that will increase their sense of self-efficacy. Those are the thinking patterns that teachers must introduce to students if they are going to leave them convinced that they have what it takes to move their *own* learning forward (Bandura, 2009).

Now, we know what you are thinking: Walking students through this three-step process before each end-of-unit exam is going to take a ton of instructional time. That is true. It will. But remember, our

Key Learnings for Our Fractions Unit:

1. I can determine a fraction by finding a part of a whole.
2. I can write mixed numbers and improper fractions by understanding the whole, or ONE.
3. I can compare fractions by
   - Thinking which is closest to 0, ½, or 1
   - Finding common denominators
   - Or noticing all the numerators are all the same
4. I can write equivalent fractions by multiplying or dividing the numerator and the denominator.
5. I can convert fractions to percent by changing the fractions to a decimal then to a percent.
6. I can identify different graphs by knowing the properties of each.

Question	Your Response
List three new things that you have learned during this unit. What do you know now that you did not know before? What can you do now that you could not do before?	I like converting fractions into decimals and then turning those decimals into percent. That is something I didn't know how to do at the beginning of this unit. I also know how to convert improper fractions into mixed numbers because I know what one whole is.
Which of the key learnings from this unit do you think you have already mastered?	I think that I have mastered the following key learnings: 1, 2, 3, 5, 6
Which of the key learnings from this unit are you still working to master?	I am struggling to master the following key learnings: 4, 7
What tips or tricks can you use when answering questions related to our key learnings on our upcoming practice test? Are there particular strategies that you can use? Phrases or acronyms that you can remember?	I know that percent circles can help me find the percent of an area on a circle graph. I always forget which numbers I am supposed to write in the boxes of a percent circle, though. I need to remind myself that the two numbers in the bottom of a percent circle should always give me the top number when I multiply them together. OR that I can figure out a missing bottom number on a percent circle by making a fraction out of the top number and the bottom number that I do have.

Figure 4.1: Sample fifth-grade student reflection before taking a practice test.

goal as instructors is not just to teach students to master the content in our required curriculum. In fact, our bet is that if you surveyed the parents of your students, you would find that they are less concerned about whether you cover your entire required curriculum and more concerned that you develop in their children both the confidence and the capacity *to act on evidence* of gaps in their current levels of mastery. Developing that confidence and capacity to act on evidence is dependent on your willingness to set time aside for students to reflect on practice attempts before final demonstrations of mastery.

Like most of the strategies we have shared throughout this book, we would argue that asking students to reflect on practice attempts should begin in the primary grades. Behaviors learned in the primary grades, after all, become habits that students carry with them through their learning careers. To help preK–2 students to reflect on their progress toward mastery through practice attempts, consider using the assessment wrappers strategy (Kerr, Hulen, Heller, & Butler, 2021). Figure 4.4, page 89, shows an example.

Question Number:	Key Learning:	While you are **TAKING** your practice test, place an X in the column below that best represents your feelings about your answer to each question.			While you are **REVIEWING** your practice test, place an X in the column below that best represents your feelings about your answer to each question.			
		This question was easy.	**I have doubts about this answer.**	**I guessed on this question.**	**I got this question right.**	**I got this question wrong. Here is why:**		
						I made a simple mistake.	I misread this question.	I need to study this again.
1	1	X			X			
2	2	X						X
3	3	X					X	
4	7		X		X			
5	6		X		X			
6	3		X				X	
7	4	X						X
8	6	X			X			
9	2, 4		X					X
10	7			X	X			
11	1	X			X			
12	5	X			X			
13	2		X					X
14	5	X			X			
15	5		X		X			

What patterns can you spot in your responses on this tracking sheet?

I noticed that I am having trouble with key learning #2. That was something that I thought I had mastered already. I'm going to want to practice a few of those questions before our unit test. I also noticed that I got both of the questions about key learning #7 correct, but I'm still going to study those. I guessed at one of the questions and got it right, but that doesn't mean I knew what I was doing on the question.

Source: Adapted from Chappuis, 2015.

Figure 4.2: Sample student template for tracking responses while taking and reviewing a practice test.

Question	Your Response
How accurate were your initial predictions? Before we took our practice test, you listed the key learnings that you thought that you had mastered already and that you were still working to master. Look back at your practice test tracking template. How did your pretest predictions match with your actual results?	I noticed that I am struggling with key learning #2. That isn't totally surprising to me, though, because I am also struggling with key learning #4. Those are related to each other. But I really thought I could do key learning #2. That's something I need more practice with.
What key learnings have you already mastered? Remember: Knowing what you have already mastered will help you to better focus your preparation time for our upcoming unit test.	I don't have to spend any time studying key learnings 1, 3, and 6. Those questions were easy for me to answer, and I got them right.
What are the most important things for you to study? Which key learnings are giving you the hardest time? How will you review these key learnings before our upcoming unit test?	I definitely need to spend time on key learnings 2 and 4. I think I'm going to review those learnings by going back to the online equivalency game that Ms. Morosini shared with us. I liked playing that, and the visuals were helpful in figuring out how mixed fractions and whole numbers matched each other.
What do you need to spend time reviewing? What kinds of simple mistakes were you making that you can quickly correct before our upcoming unit test? Which questions were you unsure of but got right on our practice test? What steps can you take to prepare for those questions on our upcoming unit test?	I made simple reading mistakes on both questions for key learning #3. I better practice those kinds of questions a little more. Something about how they are written is tripping me up.
List three things that you will do to prepare for our upcoming test: Will you review your notes? Will you attend a review session with your teacher? Will you practice with a peer during class time or recess? Will you ask for more practice problems to complete? Will you ask an adult to quiz you?	1. I'm going to use the online equivalency game that Ms. Morosini shared with us to practice mixed numbers. 2. I'm going to schedule a time to meet with a peer tutor during our school's next Power Up period. 3. I'm going to go back and do all of our homework problems for key learning #3 over again.

Source: Adapted from Chappuis, 2015.

Figure 4.3: Sample student action plan to prepare for an end-of-unit exam.

Notice that primary assessment wrappers work in much the same way as the practice test tracking templates for older students. The essential outcomes covered on the assessment are listed for students in age-appropriate language. Additionally, each question on the assessment is tied directly to the essential outcome that it is designed to assess. After completing the assessment, students are asked to color the boxes underneath each question that they answered correctly green and the boxes underneath each question they answered incorrectly red. Doing so gives preK–2 learners visual cues about their overall level of mastery. By looking for patterns on their assessment wrappers, students can spot trends in their learning—outcomes that they have successfully mastered, outcomes that they are struggling to master, and outcomes of which they show inconsistent mastery. These patterns—paired with the three simple reflection questions at the bottom of the assessment wrapper—help students develop plans to move their own learning forward.

Student name: _____

Measurement Assessment Wrapper

Directions: Review your assessment and shade the questions green that you answered correctly. Shade the questions red that you answered incorrectly.

Measuring the Length of Objects

I can accurately use a measurement tool to measure the length of an object.	Question 1	Question 2	Question 3

I can estimate the length of objects (units of inches, feet, centimeters, and meters).	Question 4	Question 5

I can measure to figure out how much longer one object is than another.	Question 6	Question 7

What have you learned so far?

_____

_____

What do you still need to learn?

_____

_____

What is your new learning plan?

_____

_____

Source: Kerr et al., 2021, p. 132.

Figure 4.4: Sample assessment wrapper for measurement.

If you are interested in using practice test tracking templates or assessment wrappers in your instruction, see the reproducible tools on pages 101–104.

Introduce Students to Logical Next Steps to Move Learning Forward

One key point worth reiterating in this chapter is that all students—regardless of their current levels of mastery—want to be successful both in and beyond school. No one, after all, wakes up hoping to fail at the most important tasks they are asked to tackle. Students who are *consistently successful* in school become confident in their ability to tackle new tasks, regardless of the circumstance. This means it is our job as educators to help students to *consistently succeed*, even in the face of academic challenge.

Sounds easy, right? Teachers in a PLC at Work know that being consistently successful starts by understanding just what it is that we are supposed to know and be able to do in any given situation. Being consistently successful also depends on the ability to assess our own progress toward mastery. It is impossible to succeed if we are not clear about what it is that we are trying to accomplish and capable of spotting the gaps between *where we currently are* and *where we want to be*. Most important, being consistently successful depends on identifying next steps worth taking to move our own learning forward. *Knowing* that you have not yet achieved your goals is not as important as *being able to do something* about it.

It is that last action—identifying next steps worth taking—that is often the greatest barrier to being successful for students with a low sense of self-efficacy. Years of struggle in school leave some students doubting their own ability to change the course of their learning. Teachers can address that paralyzing sense of self-doubt by providing students with "next-step checklists" detailing approachable actions that might be worth taking (Ferriter & Cancellieri, 2017, p. 61). Figure 4.5 shows a sample next-step checklist for a sixth-grade unit on matter.

The first column of this next-step checklist reminds students of just what it is that they are working to learn. The second column points students to sources of evidence that they can consider when trying to determine whether they have any gaps in their current levels of mastery. Successful learners are clear about what it is that they are supposed to know and be able to do and work actively to track their own progress.

It is the third column of this next-step checklist that is the most important for building a sense of self-efficacy in students. Notice that it lists several specific actions that students can take to address any gaps they spot in the evidence they have collected. These actions—watching review videos, working with peer tutors, asking specific questions in class—are not new. They are the kind of next steps that are available to most students in most classrooms. But by spelling them out specifically, teachers increase the likelihood that all learners—including those who are doubtful they have what it takes to change the course of their own learning—will take a step forward. If we believe that helping students to be consistently successful is essential, then we need to explicitly detail the pathways that learners with a high sense of self-efficacy follow naturally.

Of course, the best way to keep students from doubting their ability to create their own successes is to ensure that students build a strong sense of self-efficacy from their first days in school. While it may be too much to ask students in kindergarten through second grade to keep detailed, ongoing records of the individual outcomes that they have mastered and actions they have taken over the course of an entire unit, all students can be taught that successful learners use evidence to guide their next steps. To do so in the primary grades, consider using simple efficacy sentence starters in your classroom conversations. See the sample in figure 4.6, page 92.

Notice that these sentence starters reinforce the same efficacy pathways the next-step checklists introduce to older students. Students are encouraged to think about their current level of performance, determine what that means for them as learners, and identify a logical next step worth taking. We recommend that primary teachers develop efficacy sentence starters for an element of their required curriculum—spelling patterns, word work, or basic numeracy and computation, for example—that students revisit regularly throughout the school year. Each time students work with that element of the required curriculum—whether that work happens in large groups, smaller stations, or independently—teachers can lead students through conversations using their efficacy sentence starters. Doing

Unit: Sixth-Grade Matter

Over the past few weeks, we have been working our way through a new unit. Use this next-step checklist and reflection sheet to track your progress.

Where Am I Going?	How Am I Doing?	What Are My Next Steps?
What content and skills do I need to master during this unit? What key questions have I been wrestling with?	What evidence can I collect to track my progress toward mastering essential content and skills?	What steps can I take to continue my learning?
☐ Can I name the measurable properties of matter? ☐ Can I accurately measure the mass, volume, and density of a solid and a liquid? ☐ Can I explain how the structures of solids, liquids, and gasses are similar to or different from one another? ☐ Can I detail the effect that heat has on different states of matter?	☐ My score on Matter Unit Vocabulary Test ☐ My score on States of Matter Research Project ☐ My score on Ice Cube to Water Illustration ☐ Other evidence of your learning (questions answered in class, contributions to group projects, comparisons with the thoughts of partners)	☐ Review classroom Edpuzzle tutorials on heat and characteristic properties of matter. ☐ Meet with a peer tutor during intervention period to review my density calculations for our Mystery Liquid Lab. ☐ Use Matter Unit Quizlet to review vocabulary from this unit. ☐ Extend my learning about the impact heat has on objects by studying thermal expansion gaps in bridges and buildings. ☐ Ask this question in class to clarify something that I'm wondering or confused about: _____

↑ Questions that prompt students to think about the essential outcomes they are expected to master

↑ Evidence that students can use to determine their current levels of mastery

↑ Planning steps that students can take after identifying their current levels of mastery

Source: Adapted from Ferriter & Cancellieri, 2017, p. 44.

Figure 4.5: Sample next-step checklist for a sixth-grade unit on matter.

so teaches students the language of self-assessment and establishes taking independent action on evidence as a routine early in their school careers.

You can find reproducible templates for both the next-step checklists (page 105) and efficacy sentence starters tool (page 106) at the end of this chapter.

Develop Extension Menus for Each Unit of Study

There is something we left out of the story of James Samuelson's end-of-unit test shared at the beginning of this chapter. We have not yet disclosed his response

when his instructional coach questioned him later that week, asking, "What are your plans moving forward?" To his credit, James had a detailed plan for how he was going to intervene on behalf of the students who had failed his test. He had already sought out a colleague and asked for some tips and tricks about how to reteach the content that his students had struggled with. He had also created time within his school day to meet in smaller groups with anyone who had scored a 50 percent or less on his exam. Finally, he had rearranged his pacing guide to give himself some extra time to intervene—something that he had not expected but knew was important to do.

Sentence Starters for Primary Spelling and Word Work Reflections

Teachers—to help your students develop the efficacy skills needed to monitor their own progress and to identify next steps worth taking, it is important to help them develop the thinking patterns and language that support these behaviors. Doing so can be as simple as taping efficacy sentence starters like the ones that follow to every student's desk and using them to structure classroom conversations.

I noticed that . . . *Think: What patterns do you see in your spelling test results?*	This is important because . . . *Think: How is your learning going?*	Next, I will . . . *Think: What strategies will help you get better?*
☐ I had trouble with the _____ pattern. ☐ I mastered the _____ pattern. ☐ I had difficulty with _____. ☐ I used the _____ strategy.	☐ My list words are too hard. ☐ My list words are too easy. ☐ My words are just right. ☐ I need more help with _____.	☐ Practice with the _____ strategy that we learned in class. ☐ Review word patterns that I had trouble with. ☐ Ask a friend to help me study. ☐ Ask for help from my teacher.

Figure 4.6: Sample efficacy sentence starters for primary students.

Can you spot what is missing from James's plans? While he has carefully thought through the next steps that he plans to take with the students who failed his exam, he makes no mention of the next steps that he plans to take with the eight students in his class who aced it the first time around.

To experienced educators, that is not totally surprising. Whether we like it or not, many teachers and collaborative teams continue to think that *intervention* means helping struggling students to master grade-level curricula (Roberts, 2019). As a result, intervention efforts in schools—like those in James's classroom—are often centered on providing remedial instruction in foundational skills or extra practice with grade-level essentials. And, in many ways, these efforts make sense. After all, students *do* have to master grade-level essentials to be successful in school—and allowing struggling learners to move forward without mastering those essentials is irresponsible and will leave them behind in future courses of study (Williams & Hierck, 2015).

The problem with thinking of intervention as helping struggling students to succeed is that we often forget that the primary purpose of PLCs is to ensure that *all students*—including those who are working *beyond* our expectations—learn at the highest levels (Roberts, 2019). When we define intervention as any effort to help struggling learners, we unintentionally prioritize our work with students who need additional support (PLC critical question 3) and overlook the needs of students who have attained proficiency (PLC critical question 4). What's more, because students are unique individuals with differing skill sets, every student is likely to need *both* intervention and extension at differing points over the course of a school year (Roberts, 2019).

Overlooking the importance of extension in our intervention plans can also have negative efficacy implications for proficient students. Remember, self-efficacy means having "capabilities to organize and execute the courses of action required to manage prospective situations" (Bandura, 1995, p. 2). For proficient students, executing a course of action most often means asking, "How can I extend my learning after I have mastered important outcomes?" If teachers fail to help proficient students realize that academic growth and discovery are a continuous and ongoing process, they begin to think that learning stops once they have mastered the grade-level curriculum. High-functioning teams, then, recognize that using the PLC at Work process to build efficacy in learners starts only after we develop strategies that leave *every student*—including the highest achievers—convinced that there are next steps worth taking.

One of the simplest steps that teams can take to help their highest achievers identify next steps worth taking is to develop extension menus for each unit of study. Developing an extension menu starts by first understanding the four main strategies that collaborative teams take to extend learning (DuFour et al., 2016; Roberts, 2019).

1. **Asking students to demonstrate mastery at levels beyond grade-level proficiency:** Grade-level curricula are often spiraled—introducing students in different grade levels to similar concepts at increasing levels of complexity. To extend learning, collaborative teams can create tasks that ask proficient students to wrestle with these spiraled concepts and to demonstrate mastery at levels that go beyond grade-level expectations.

2. **Giving students opportunities to study nonessential curricula:** When answering the first critical question of learning in a PLC—What do we want students to know and be able to do?—teams generate lists of *need* to knows and *nice* to knows. The outcomes on need-to-know lists become the grade-level essentials that all students are expected to master. Teachers can introduce the nonessential outcomes on nice-to-know lists to proficient students as part of extension efforts.

3. **Teaching students above grade-level curricula:** Collaborative teams in PLCs understand that learning is often progressive. The concepts and skills that students must master this year are foundational to understanding the concepts and skills that they will be asked to master next year. To develop extensions, then, learning teams often create tasks that ask students to wrestle with content that will be introduced to learners in subsequent grade levels.

4. **Introducing students to real-life examples of essential outcomes in action:** For students, engagement in schools often

depends on understanding why the learning outcomes they are being introduced to matter. Learning teams can turn this need for relevance into extension tasks by asking students to spot places where grade-level concepts and skills are playing a role in life beyond schools or to use the knowledge that they have already mastered to solve real-world problems.

Once teams understand the strategies that teachers can take to extend learning, they can work together to generate one task that falls into each of the four categories. Those tasks can then be shared with all students who demonstrate mastery of grade-level essentials as an extension menu. Teachers can either assign specific tasks to individual learners based on need or allow their proficient students to make individual choices about which extension tasks they would most like to complete.

Figure 4.7 (page 94) is an example of an extension menu that social studies students who are examining the ways that conflict, compromise, and negotiation have shaped the United States could be asked to complete.

Notice that this extension menu explicitly names the type of extension students can choose to work on. That is deliberate. By explicitly naming categories of extensions on an extension menu, teachers remind students of the kinds of steps that high achievers take when moving beyond basic expectations. From an efficacy-building standpoint, knowledge of options is essential. Sometimes, students struggle to take next steps simply because they have no real sense of just what taking a next step can look like. In classrooms where teachers use extension menus frequently, high-performing students learn that there are always learning opportunities available and that those opportunities generally fall into four categories: (1) working beyond proficiency, (2) studying nonessential curricula, (3) studying above grade-level curricula, or (4) studying real-life examples of essential outcomes in action.

We also suggest that collaborative teams *begin* their unit planning by developing extension menus. Doing so helps to ensure that planning for extension does not become a "fly by the seat of your pants" experience (Roberts, 2019, p. 38). Just as important, planning

Extension Menu: Conflict, Compromise, and Negotiation

Over the last two weeks, we have been studying the role that conflict, compromise, and negotiation play in shaping the United States. Specifically, we have looked at how the Civil Rights movement influenced the steps that we have taken toward racial equity in America.

You have demonstrated mastery of this topic already in class. To extend your learning, choose one of the tasks below to complete and design a strategy for sharing your learning with your teacher.

Working Beyond Grade-Level Proficiency	Studying Nonessential Curricula
During this unit, you had to show me that you could identify the positive impact that individual events in the Civil Rights movement had on improving life for marginalized groups in the United States. What I didn't ask you to do is to determine whether individual events in the Civil Rights movement had any unintended consequences—things that didn't quite go as planned or that led to future problems. Go back to our unit and find an event that we studied that had unintended consequences that led to future conflicts, compromises, or negotiations.	During this unit, we studied major events in the Civil Rights movement that happened at the national level. But the fact of the matter is that there were events in the Civil Rights movement that happened right here in our state. Research some of those events. Find three, summarize them, and rank them in order of importance from "Had the least impact on the marginalized people of our state" to "Had the greatest impact on the marginalized people of our state."
Studying Above-Grade-Level Curricula	**Studying Real-Life Examples of Essential Outcomes in Action**
Because our course is focused on U.S. history, we have spent most of our time concentrating on the fight for civil rights in our own nation. Next year, you will take a course in world history. Find another historical example of marginalized people fighting for civil rights that has happened in another country. Compare that fight to the Civil Rights movement in the United States. How were they similar to one another? How were they different? Remember: People aren't *just* marginalized because of the color of their skin. There are lots of reasons that people have been discriminated against.	In the spring of 2020, America saw huge protests over police treatment of people of color. Led by the Black Lives Matter movement, these protests sought to raise awareness about the differences between policing practices in Black and White communities. Research the Black Lives Matter movement: 1. What are its stated goals? 2. Who are its leaders? 3. What successes has it had in improving life for marginalized people? 4. What would critics say about the movement?

Figure 4.7: Sample extension menu for social studies unit on conflict, compromise, and negotiation.

for extension often results in much more meaningful learning experiences and higher levels of achievement for all students because it allows teams to clarify a vision for beyond-grade-level performance and then scaffold instruction to allow all students—regardless of ability—to access that instruction (Tomlinson, 2015).

You can find a template for creating your own extension menu (page 107) and a reproducible copy of an extension menu (page 108) at the end of this chapter.

Help Older Students Put Grades in Context

In a seminal article written for *Educational Leadership* in 2012, Grant Wiggins made a surprising argument about the way educators in schools evaluate students. He writes, "The most ubiquitous form of evaluation, grading, is so much a part of the school landscape that we easily overlook its utter uselessness as actionable feedback. Grades are here to stay, no doubt—but that doesn't mean we should rely on them as a major source of feedback" (Wiggins, 2012, p. 16). Chances are that readers of this text would universally agree that Wiggins is right when he describes grades as an utterly useless form of actionable feedback. And chances are that those same readers could list all the ways that traditional grading practices hurt students—particularly those who struggle in school.

But Wiggins is likely also right *that grades are here to stay*—at least for the immediate future. Even as we work to reimagine what teaching and learning should look like in a modern world, most schools and districts still require classroom teachers to use letter and number grades to assess student learning. Just as importantly, many parents—having worked their way through a school system where number and letter grades were ubiquitous—still expect their students to be graded. Whether we like it or not, grades remain the norm rather than the exception to the rule, and students still define themselves—and each other—by the grades they receive. Each individual mark, then—positive or negative—reinforces a student's sense of academic efficacy.

In their work to ensure higher levels of learning for all students, the teachers at Fern Creek High School in Louisville, Kentucky, decided to change the role that grades play in the lives of their learners. Those efforts started when they instituted regularly scheduled six-week grade check-ins. During those grade check-ins, every student is expected to fill out a self-reporting tool detailing the grades they have earned up until that point in the quarter. Figure 4.8 (page 96) shows an example.

The goal of the first page of this self-reporting tool is to help students look beyond the single overall grade that is most often reported as a demonstration of mastery in high school classes. Instead, students at Fern Creek collect lots of scores, including overall averages and current letter grades as well as percentages for each of the individual topics they studied during the six-week period students are reflecting on. Finally, students are asked to color code the grades that they have earned, integrating visual mastery cues into their self-reporting tool. By asking students to record and review multiple grades on their six-week grade reflections, the teachers at Fern Creek High School have turned individual scores into actionable information that students can use to identify patterns in their performance.

In fact, the entire second page of the Fern Creek Student Self-Reporting Tool is designed to help students act on the evidence that they have collected. Figure 4.9 (page 97) shows a sample of the second page of the tool.

Notice that once students have had a chance to think through the individual learning targets that they have already mastered and that they are still working to master, they are asked to identify a next step worth taking. Those next steps include retaking assessments, getting help with organization and note-taking, and attending review sessions with teachers or peer tutors. By asking students to think about next steps, Fern Creek High School teachers are reminding their students that scores earned are not *permanent definitions of who a student is as a learner*. Instead, scores earned are *indicators of current levels of mastery that can be changed* through the individual choices and actions of learners. In many ways, by using six-week grade check-ins to put marks earned into context for their learners, Fern Creek High School has maximized the value of grades as a shorthand tool for providing feedback by sending consistent messages to students that grades reflect "where you are in your learning journey—and where is always temporary" (Guskey, 2019).

We do not endorse a one-size-fits-all approach. The format for the six-week grade reflection looks different in the English department, the science department, and so on. The staff at Fern Creek understand the idea of autonomy with accountability. Teams are held accountable that they will invest time, energy, and passion to this important task that occurs every six weeks, but the format they design does not have to look the same from department to department. There is clarity throughout the school that this is not only an expectation, but teachers understand the why behind the effort. They want students to become more reflective and invested in their own learning.

If you are interested in replicating this practice in your own classroom or building, you can use the reproducible six-week student self-reporting tool on page 109.

Directions: Please take out your grade sheet and use it to fill out the following self-reporting tables. Then, use the information that you have gathered to plan next steps worth taking to improve your learning before the end of the quarter.

Step 1: Look at your overall grades for the last six weeks.

Source of Information	Your Score	Source of Information	Your Score
Overall Percentage in Class		Current Letter Grade in Class	
Summative Assessment Percentage		Weekly Performance Percentage	
Weekly ACT Practice Percentage		ACT Growth Percentage	

Step 2: Explore the grades that you have earned over the last six weeks by the topics we have covered.

Topic Covered	Your Score	Topic Covered	Your Score
Pre-Algebra Percentage		Elementary Algebra Percentage	
The highest score that I earned on this topic was: The lowest score that I earned on this topic was:		The highest score that I earned on this topic was: The lowest score that I earned on this topic was:	
Intermediate Algebra Percentage		Coordinate Geometry Percentage	
The highest score that I earned on this topic was: The lowest score that I earned on this topic was:		The highest score that I earned on this topic was: The lowest score that I earned on this topic was:	

Step 3: Review all the marks that you have recorded on your self-reporting tool. While reviewing:

- ☐ Shade any score that is 80 percent or higher **GREEN**.
- ☐ Shade any score that is a 70 percent to 79 percent **YELLOW**.
- ☐ Shade any score that is below a 70 percent **RED**.

Source: Adapted from © 2017 by Fern Creek High School. Used with permission.

Figure 4.8: Sample first page of the student self-reporting tool—Six-week grade check-in.

Final Review:

Question to Consider	Your Response
What learning targets have you mastered in the last six weeks?	
What learning targets are you still working to master?	
Are you satisfied with your overall grade in this class? Why or why not?	
What patterns can you spot in the kinds of tasks that you are earning high or low marks? What explains those patterns?	

Next Steps:

Please place a **checkmark** next to any and all interventions that you think may help you recover some of your scores. Provide a one- or two-sentence explanation about **why** each specific intervention will help you.

	Retake an assessment: You understand your mistakes, and you are ready to try again.
Your Reasoning:	
	Take preventative measures: You would like to take extra steps to prevent low scores to begin with. These steps could include learning more about note-taking strategies, getting help with organization, or completing extra practice activities on your own time.
Your Reasoning:	
	Get small-group or individual after-school help: You are struggling to understand a concept or a skill and would like to come after school for a reteaching session.
Your Reasoning:	
	Other: You have an idea for improving your work, and you would like to suggest it to me.
Your Reasoning:	

Source: Adapted from © 2017 by Fern Creek High School. Used with permission.

Figure 4.9: Sample second page of student self-reporting tool—six-week grade check-in.

Recommendations for Getting Started

As one of the first researchers to describe the characteristics of effective feedback to learners, Royce Sadler has become a powerful voice on the role that feedback can play in building a sense of self-efficacy in students. His work—particularly a paper written in 1989 titled "Formative Assessment and the Design of Instructional Systems"—continues to inform many of today's leading voices on grading and feedback in schools. In that piece, Sadler argues that a student needs more than just a summary grade from a teacher to "develop expertise intelligently" (Sadler, 1989, p. 121). To develop expertise intelligently, the learner must:

> (a). possess a concept of the *standard* (or goal, or reference level) being aimed for, (b). compare the *actual* (or current) *level of performance* with the standard, and (c). engage in appropriate *action* which leads to some closure of the gap. (Sadler, 1989, p. 121, emphasis in original)

John Hattie and Shirley Clarke (2019) echoed Sadler's criteria for effective feedback thirty years later, when they argue that "improving learning through feedback" depends on "providing feedback which leads to students recognizing their next steps and how to take them" (p. 9).

What does that mean for classroom teachers? It means that our goal should be to structure feedback experiences *that encourage students to act* on evidence that they collect about their current levels of mastery and that emphasize the notion that continued growth is a function of efforts taken instead of innate ability. Here are a few recommendations for creating those kinds of feedback experiences in your classroom: (1) limit your corrective feedback to students, (2) ask students to describe changes without requiring that they make the changes, and (3) allow frequent technology use.

Limit Your Corrective Feedback to Students

Have you ever caught yourself trying to correct every single mistake on a task turned in by one of your students? This is a trap most teachers fall into while grading assignments. When we see mistakes—no matter how small they may be—we want to point them out to students so that they can either correct them in the moment or know better for the next time. As a result, teachers spend hours grading work and then return papers to students that are covered in corrections. Have you ever been annoyed while handing back assignments because students barely looked at any of your feedback? We have all had moments where the time we spent giving feedback felt wasted because students did nothing with the suggestions we offered.

In those moments, it is tempting to question student intentions. "They don't care about improving," we may think. "They just care about chasing points." Instead, we should be questioning our decision to provide students with so much feedback to begin with. The goal should not be "to provide all the correctives necessary to make the work perfect," explains assessment expert Jan Chappuis (2012). Instead, the goal should be to "provide as much guidance as the student can reasonably act on" (Chappuis, 2012). What is more, we must provide students with *the time to act* on any feedback we provide. "Feedback 'so they know better next time' is a waste of energy" (Brookhart, 2012). Giving students too much feedback and not enough time to act does little to help learners in the long run. Instead, it leaves students intellectually paralyzed—unsure of where to begin and doubting their own ability to succeed.

Ask Students to Describe Changes Without Requiring That They Make the Changes

Even if we do not overwhelm our students with feedback, some learners are going to be uninterested in taking next steps to improve their work. For students, taking next steps to improve their work means *doing more work*—and doing more work can be a frustrating process for a learner who has already invested a significant amount of time into creating a final product. Think back to Isabel—the third-grade learner spotlighted at the start of chapter 2. Simply creating the state pamphlet assigned to her proved to be a real challenge. Our guess is that by the time Isabel was finished with her pamphlet, she was ready to move on—and if her teacher had asked her to change her final product, Isabel would have lost her patience!

The solution is, at the end of some important assignments, ask students to describe changes they *would* make to their work—but do not require them to make any of the changes that they identify (Wiliam, 2016). That may seem counterintuitive at first. After all, what is the use of identifying potential improvements if you are never going to make them? Remember, however, that the goal when giving feedback is not to *change the work*. The goal when giving feedback is to *change the learner* (Wiliam, 2016). As Dylan Wiliam explains, the purpose of creating opportunities for reflection without requiring subsequent revision is to develop "the student's own critical eye" because "once a student has that, feedback from others becomes less and less necessary" (Wiliam, 2016).

Allow Frequent Technology Use

The challenge of getting students to take next steps to improve their work is hardly new. In fact, regardless of the quality of the final product that they produce, most students are just as likely to tell you that their work is not in need of revision as they are to point out places where they can make changes. Why are students so averse to taking next steps to move both themselves and their final products forward? Because the transaction costs of making revisions almost always outweigh the perceived benefits that come along with improving. Stated another way, the incentive to change is outweighed by the time, energy, and effort that those changes will take (Cancellieri, 2020b).

The good news is that technology can reduce the transaction costs of almost any task. That means if you are willing to allow students to create their final products using digital tools, you are more likely to see them receptive to the idea of identifying places where they can move their work forward (Cancellieri, 2020b). Essays are far easier to revise when they are written in Google Docs than the same essays written on notebook paper; science fair projects are far easier to polish when they are created in Google Slides than the same projects pasted onto foam display boards; and state pamphlet projects are far easier to enhance if they are created using simple video editing tools than the same projects crafted by hand. If we are genuinely interested in seeing students act to improve their own learning, we need to do all that we can to make *taking action* easier for students.

Concluding Thoughts

Highly functioning teams in PLCs are committed to the notion that the choices they make to respond to the unique learning needs of students cannot be left to chance. Teachers in PLCs recognize that their obligation goes beyond simply presenting a coherent lesson and then assessing whether students have mastered the content covered in that lesson. Instead, teachers in PLCs see it as their obligation to *take deliberate action* to ensure that all students learn at the highest levels.

That obligation is fully expressed in the third and fourth critical questions of a PLC that collaborative teams use to guide their work (DuFour et al., 2016): How will we respond when some students do not learn? and How will we extend the learning for students who are already proficient? When teams work together to develop systematic responses to address the identified needs of every student, they create spaces where all learners can succeed. Furthermore, when teams work together to develop systematic responses to successfully address the identified needs of every student, they gather tangible evidence that they are capable of driving change, regardless of circumstance (Donohoo, 2017). Finally, teams with a high rate of confidence in their own ability to move learning forward regardless of circumstance tend to foster higher rates of confidence in their learners—leaving *students* convinced that they can do well in school, too (Donohoo, 2017).

For Hattie (2018), gathering tangible evidence that they have what it takes to drive change regardless of circumstance builds the collective efficacy of collaborative teams. Collective teacher efficacy, he explains:

> Isn't just growth mindset. It's not just rah-rah thinking; it's not just, "Oh—we can make a difference!" But it is the combined belief that it is us that causes learning. It is not the students. It's not the students from particular social backgrounds. It's not all the barriers out there. Because when you fundamentally believe that you can make the difference, and then you feed it with the evidence that you are, that is dramatically powerful.

It is just as important for students to fundamentally believe in their own ability to respond when they have not yet learned essential content, skills, or behaviors and when they are already working beyond grade-level expectations. Students who believe in their own ability to respond approach new situations with optimism and assurance. They are more persistent, more likely to set challenging goals for themselves, and more willing to take intellectual risks because they recognize that they really can be successful.

We argue that helping students develop these self-efficacious behaviors cannot be left to chance.

Teachers and collaborative teams must design and deliver learning experiences that encourage students to take deliberate action to move their own learning forward. That work may feel tedious at first—after all, students in traditional schools are rarely asked to reflect on their current progress toward mastery and then choose logical next steps worth taking. But when students succeed at both monitoring and mastering appropriately challenging goals because of their own efforts and actions, they develop the confidence necessary for succeeding both in and beyond school.

Practice Test Tracking Template

Directions for teachers: To develop a tracking template for an upcoming practice test, you will need to: (1) create a numbered list of all key learnings for your current unit of study in the empty box under step one and (2) align each question on your practice test to one of your key learnings in the second column under step two.

Student Name: _____

Step 1: Complete Before You Take Your Practice Test

Directions: Review the key learnings for our _____ unit. While reviewing, complete the following reflection questions.

KEY LEARNINGS FOR OUR UNIT ON _____

Question	Your Response
List three new things that you have learned during this unit. What do you know now that you did not know before? What can you do now that you could not do before?	
Which of the key learnings from this unit do you think you have already mastered?	I think that I have mastered the following key learnings:
Which of the key learnings from this unit are you still working to master?	I am struggling to master the following key learnings:
What tips or tricks can you use when answering questions related to our key learnings on our upcoming practice test? Are there particular strategies that you can use? Phrases or acronyms that you can remember?	

Step 2: Complete During Your Practice Test and While We Are Reviewing Answers Together in Class

Directions: Use the left-hand side of the table to keep track of the questions that are hard for you to answer on our practice test. Then, use the right-hand side of the table to develop a plan for yourself while we are scoring our practice test together in class.

		While you are **TAKING** your practice test, place an X in the column below that best represents your feelings about your answer to each question.			While you are **REVIEWING** your practice test, place an X in the column below that best represents your feelings about your answer to each question.			
Question Number:	Key Learning:	This question was easy.	I have doubts about this answer.	I guessed on this question.	I got this question right.	I got this question wrong. Here is why:		
						I made a simple mistake.	I misread this question.	I need to study this again.
1								
2								
3								
4								
5								
6								
7								
8								
9								
10								
11								
12								
13								
14								
15								

What patterns can you spot in your responses on this tracking sheet?

Step 3: Complete After You Take Your Practice Test

Directions: Answer the following questions to build a study plan for your upcoming end-of-unit test.

Question	Your Response
How accurate were your initial predictions? Before we took our practice test, you listed the key learnings that you thought that you had mastered already and that you were still working to master. Look back at your practice test tracking template. How did your pretest predictions match with your actual results?	
What key learnings have you already mastered? Remember: Knowing what you have already mastered will help you to better focus your preparation time for our upcoming unit test.	
What are the most important things for you to study? Which key learnings are giving you the hardest time? How will you review these key learnings before our upcoming unit test?	
What do you need to spend time reviewing? Which key learnings confused you on our practice test? What kinds of simple mistakes were you making that you can quickly correct before our upcoming unit test? Which questions were you unsure of on our practice test? What steps can you take to prepare for those questions on our upcoming unit test?	
List three things that you will do to prepare for our upcoming test: Will you review your notes? Will you attend a review session with your teacher? Will you practice with a peer during class time or recess? Will you ask for more practice problems to complete? Will you ask an adult to quiz you?	

Source: Questions adapted from Chappuis, J. (2015). Seven strategies of assessment for learning. New York: Pearson Education.

Assessment Wrapper—Second-Grade Measurement

Student name: _____

Directions: Review your assessment and shade the questions green that you answered correctly. Shade the questions red that you answered incorrectly.

Measuring the Length of Objects

I can accurately use a measurement tool to measure the length of an object.	Question 1	Question 2	Question 3

I can estimate the length of objects (units of inches, feet, centimeters, and meters).	Question 4	Question 5

I can measure to figure out how much longer one object is than another.	Question 6	Question 7

What have you learned so far?

What do you still need to learn?

What is your new learning plan?

Using Next-Step Checklists to Help Students Take Next Steps

Self-efficacy means believing in one's ability to succeed in any situation. Self-efficacy develops when students experience success in overcoming gaps in their own learning. To help your students overcome gaps in their own learning, consider creating progress checklists that (1) remind students of the outcomes that they are expected to master, (2) detail sources of evidence that students can use to identify gaps in their current levels of mastery, and (3) outline specific sets of next steps that students can take to close the gap between where they are and where they hope to be as learners. Use this template to create a progress checklist for one of your upcoming units of study.

Where Am I Going? What content and skills do I need to master during this unit? What key questions have I been wrestling with?	How Am I Doing? What evidence can I collect to track my progress toward mastering essential content and skills?	What Are My Next Steps? What steps can I take to continue my learning?
☐	☐	☐
☐	☐	☐
☐	☐	☐
☐	☐	☐

Source: Adapted from Ferriter, W. M., & Cancellieri, P. J. (2017). Creating a culture of feedback: Solutions for creating the learning spaces students deserve. *Bloomington, IN: Solution Tree Press.*

Checklist Development Directions for Learning Teams

1. In the **Where Am I Going?** column, list three to five essential outcomes for this upcoming unit of study that are written in student-friendly language. Consider creating questions that students can answer with a clear YES or NO response.

2. In the **How Am I Doing?** column, list three to five tasks that students can use as evidence to assess their own progress toward mastering the essential outcomes covered on this checklist.

3. In the **What Are My Next Steps?** column, list three to five specific actions that students can take to move their own learning forward. These actions should be clearly understood by students and require no additional direction from the teacher in the classroom.

Creating Efficacy Sentence Starters for Primary Students

To help primary students develop the efficacy skills needed to monitor their own progress and to identify next steps worth taking, it is important to consistently reinforce the thinking patterns and language that support these behaviors. Doing so can be as simple as taping efficacy sentence starters to every student's desk and using them to structure classroom conversations.

I noticed that . . .
Think: What patterns do you see in your test results?
☐ I had trouble with _____ .
☐ I mastered _____ .
☐ I had difficulty with _____ .
☐ I used the _____ strategy.
This is important because . . .
Think: How is your learning going?
☐ I am still working to learn _____ .
☐ I need something more challenging to study.
☐ I have gotten better at _____ .
☐ I need more help with _____ .
Next, I will . . .
Think: What strategies will help you get better?
☐ Practice with the _____ strategy that we learned in class.
☐ Review _____ that I had trouble with.
☐ Ask a friend to help me study.
☐ Ask for help from my teacher.

Developing an Extension Menu for a Unit of Study

Directions for teachers: Begin planning for your next unit of study by developing four extension tasks that proficient students can complete once they have demonstrated mastery of your grade-level essential learnings.

Type of Extension	Team-Developed Task
Demonstrating mastery at levels beyond grade-level proficiency: Grade-level curricula are often spiraled—introducing students in different grade levels to similar concepts at increasing levels of complexity. To extend learning, collaborative teams can create tasks that ask proficient students to wrestle with these spiraled concepts and to demonstrate mastery at levels that go beyond grade-level expectations.	
Studying nonessential curricula: When answering the first critical question of learning in a PLC—What do we want our students to know and be able to do?—teams generate lists of need to knows and nice to knows. The outcomes on need-to-know lists become the grade-level essentials that all students are expected to master. The nonessential outcomes on nice-to-know lists can be introduced to proficient students as a part of extension efforts.	
Demonstrating mastery at levels beyond grade-level proficiency: Grade-level curricula are often spiraled—introducing students in different grade levels to similar concepts at increasing levels of complexity. To extend learning, teams can create tasks that ask proficient students to wrestle with these spiraled concepts and to demonstrate mastery at levels that go beyond grade-level expectations.	
Studying real-life examples of essential outcomes in action: For students, engagement in school often depends on understanding why the learning outcomes that they are being introduced to matter. Learning teams can turn this need for relevance into extension tasks by asking students to spot places where grade-level concepts and skills are playing a role in life beyond schools or to use the knowledge that they have already mastered to solve real-life problems.	

Extension Menu for Upcoming Unit of Study

Student name: _____ **Unit:** _____

Directions for students: Once you have demonstrated mastery of the essential outcomes in our current unit of study, extend your learning by completing one of the tasks in the following menu. When you are finished, design a strategy for sharing what you have learned with your teacher.

Working Beyond Grade-Level Proficiency	Studying Nonessential Curricula
Studying Above Grade-Level Curricula	**Studying Real-Life Examples of Essential Outcomes in Action**

Planning Questions to Consider:

1. Which task do you most want to complete? Why?

2. Brainstorm three different strategies for sharing what you learn with your teacher:

3. Which of those strategies will be the easiest to complete? The hardest? Why?

4. Which strategy will give you the best chance of showing what you have learned?

Student Self-Reporting Six-Week Grade Check-In

Student name: _____ Unit: _____

Directions for students: Please take out your grade sheet and use it to fill out the following self-reporting template. Then, use the information that you have gathered to plan next steps worth taking to improve your learning before the end of the quarter.

Step 1: Look at your overall grades for the last six weeks.

Source of Information	Your Score	Source of Information	Your Score
Overall Percentage in Class		**Current Letter Grade in Class**	
Summative Assessment Percentage		**Weekly Performance Percentage**	
Other		**Other**	

Step 2: Explore the grades you have earned over the last six weeks by the topics we have covered.

Topic Covered	Your Score	Topic Covered	Your Score
Topic 1:		**Topic 2:**	
The highest score that I earned on this topic was: The lowest score that I earned on this topic was:		The highest score that I earned on this topic was: The lowest score that I earned on this topic was:	
Topic 3:		**Topic 4:**	
The highest score that I earned on this topic was: The lowest score that I earned on this topic was:		The highest score that I earned on this topic was: The lowest score that I earned on this topic was:	

Step 3: Review all the marks that you have recorded on your self-reporting tool. While reviewing:

- ☐ Shade any score that is 80 percent or higher **GREEN**.
- ☐ Shade any score that is a 70 percent to 79 percent **YELLOW**.
- ☐ Shade any score that is below a 70 percent **RED**.

page 1 of 2

Final Review

Question to Consider	Your Response
What learning targets have you mastered in the last six weeks?	
What learning targets are you still working to master?	
Are you satisfied with your overall grade in this class? Why or why not?	
What patterns can you spot in the kinds of tasks that you are earning high or low marks in? What explains those patterns?	

Next Steps

Please place a **checkmark** next to any interventions you think may help you recover some of your scores. Provide a one- or two-sentence explanation about **why** each specific intervention will help you.

	Retake an assessment: You understand your mistakes, and you are ready to try again.
Your reasoning:	

	Take preventative measures: You would like to take extra steps to prevent low scores to begin with. These steps could include learning more about note-taking strategies, getting help with organization, or completing extra practice activities on your own time.
Your reasoning:	

	Get small-group or individual after-school help: You are struggling to understand a concept or a skill and would like to come after school for a reteaching session.
Your reasoning:	

	Other: You have an idea for improving your work, and you would like to suggest it to me.
Your reasoning:	

page 2 of 2

Epilogue

The central contention throughout this book has been that collaborative teams need to extend their work with the four critical questions of the PLC at Work process into their classrooms and to share this work with their students. It is one thing for the adults in a school to have a mission, a vision, a set of commitments, and measurable goals to track progress toward mastery. But powerful classroom communities develop only after the adults in a building create compelling ways to communicate these ideas to their students. Think about it this way.

- If we believe that it is important for teams to set goals, then shouldn't goal setting be a part of the work we do with students?

- If we believe that it is important for teams to be clear on what is essential, then wouldn't it be just as important for students to understand what is essential?

- If we believe that it is important for teams to examine and analyze data, then shouldn't we give students chances to examine and analyze their own learning data?

- If we believe that it is important for teams to take action after collecting evidence of mastery, then shouldn't we help students take action after collecting evidence of their own mastery?

- If we believe that collective efficacy is an influential factor for the success of collaborative teams, then wouldn't we implement strategies that encourage the development of efficacy in our students?

Stated another way, if we endorse the fundamental assumption that schools are not built to ensure *that students are taught*, but instead to ensure *that students learn*, we need to work with our colleagues to carefully design classroom practices that support the principles of learning that we believe in. Doing so will result in more confident, persistent students who are willing to take risks and who are more likely to stick with tasks even when they are difficult.

But don't just take our word for it. Instead, look closely at the research around student self-efficacy that Marzano, Pickering, and Heflebower (2011) detail in *The Highly Engaged Classroom*. To Marzano and his colleagues (2011), teachers who build high levels of efficacy in learners help students set personal academic goals and track their own progress over time, ask students to examine their effort and preparation for assignments and assessments, avoid giving students verbal feedback that could create a fixed mindset, and use stories and quotes to promote a growth mindset in students. These simple, commonsense practices—which are evident in the principles of learning that so many teachers acknowledge as axioms in our profession—have an effect size of .82, translating into an expected 29 percentile point gain for learners (Marzano et al., 2011).

That makes connecting our instructional decisions to the principles of learning that we all believe in one of the most important steps that we can take as practitioners.

Tips for Getting Started

We hope that the research shared in the previous four chapters has left you with the evidence you need to find the through lines running between the principles of learning that you believe in, the work that you do with your colleagues, and the work that you do with your students. The fact of the matter is that the same four critical questions that lead to higher levels of learning and efficacy for *teachers* can also lead to higher levels of learning and efficacy for *students*. It is also our hope that we have provided enough examples from the field to get every team started. Finally, we hope that you see the actions suggested in this book as not only doable but as imperative for creating more confident, self-aware students.

We do, however, have a few final suggestions to offer.

Start Small

Within this book, we have shared more than a dozen different teaching strategies that are tied to the four critical questions of learning in a PLC at Work. Our goal in sharing all these strategies is not to suggest that you drop everything and find ways to integrate every practice into the work you are doing with your students. Instead, our goal in sharing all these strategies is to make sure that every reader finds *something* to quickly and easily embrace.

So, instead of worrying about all the things you could be doing with your students, find the one strategy in this text that is the perfect starting point for you and your collaborative team. Maybe your team is in the middle of identifying essential outcomes with one another. If so, then using unit overview sheets (page 77) or primary progress tracking cards (page 79) to communicate outcomes to your students might be the first step that you take to integrate efficacy-building into your instruction. Or perhaps your team is digging deep into interventions and extensions this year. If so, then asking students to complete practice test tracking templates (page 101) or to use efficacy sentence starters (page 106) could be worth exploring.

By closely tying the work that you are doing with your professional team to the work you are doing with your students, you are more likely to find value in the time, energy, and effort that it takes to make new

strategies a part of your instructional routine. That work, after all, rests on the same through lines. And by limiting your change efforts to one new practice per school year, you are more likely to sustain your attempts to integrate efficacy-building into your classroom from September through June. In the end, it is important to remember that adding a single new practice to your pedagogical bag of tricks will have a greater long-term impact on student learning than trying to tackle lots of new strategies and then giving up because you feel overwhelmed by all the changes that you are trying to make at once.

Work Fast and Finish

Another common barrier to change on learning teams is the tendency to want a product or a practice to be perfect before using it with students. As a result, teams can spend hours—even weeks—working on the same lesson plan, curriculum map, common formative assessment, or intervention activity. We nitpick the language in our directions or in the questions that we are asking students to respond to. We tinker with the formatting of our documents, debating the fonts that we are using or whether an individual tool is best presented to students in portrait or landscape view. We look through clip art galleries for the best graphics to add to our final products, convinced that somehow, interesting graphics make a final product more useful or engaging to our students. The result is that teachers walk out of collaborative team meetings doubting whether it is even possible to get anything done with one another.

Overcoming this barrier starts when teams make a commitment to work fast and finish. Trying to design a set of exemplars or a single-point rubric with one another? Want to create an assessment wrapper (page 104) or a next-step checklist (page 105) for an upcoming unit of study? Set a timer for sixty minutes and have it finished before your weekly meeting ends. Will your final products be perfect? Probably not—but they don't have to be. You have plenty of time to revise and polish as you create similar documents for subsequent units of study. What is most important is that your team members leave each meeting convinced that integrating efficacy-building practices into instruction is doable—and nothing will leave you more convinced that efficacy-building practices are doable than *getting something done.*

Use the Reproducibles in This Book

You can also save yourself time by using the reproducibles included in this book. Visit **go.SolutionTree .com/PLCbooks** to download these free reproducibles. While they may not be formatted exactly as you would like them to be, *they are already finished.* That means you can begin using them in the classroom with your students immediately. As you see how your students respond to the files as they are, you can note changes that you would like to make moving forward. And as you become convinced that using the PLC at Work process to build efficacy in students is a concept worth embracing, you won't mind the time that it takes to create your own tools to support the strategies that you most believe in. After all, those tools will help you to connect what you believe about learning to the work that you are asking your students to complete. Nothing could be more rewarding for a classroom teacher.

Do This Work With Your Collaborative Team

Look back at the three suggestions we just covered. They all call on members of collaborative teams to work together to integrate student efficacy-building practices into their instruction. See, for those of us who believe in the power of PLCs, working collaboratively to identify strategies that help more students learn at higher levels has always been what matters most. Sure, individual teachers can integrate efficacy-building practices into their own classrooms and have a positive impact on the learners they serve. But how much more powerful would those efforts be if they sat at the center of the regular work done by collaborative teams across an entire school building?

Create Capable and Competent Learners

Our deepest hope is that you will set aside some time with your colleagues this year to turn the theories around both professional learning and self-efficacy into instructional practices that play a central role in the work you do with your learners. Doing so will leave every student in your classroom better prepared to succeed in a constantly changing world where reflection, adaptation, and resilience are essential traits. More important, doing so will leave every student in your classroom convinced that he or she really is a capable and competent learner. None of the practices we are proposing that you wrestle with are radical. They just rely on your willingness to look at schooling through the eyes of your students. We wish you well on that remarkable journey!

REFERENCES AND RESOURCES

Ackerman, C. E. (2020, December 21). *What is self-efficacy theory in psychology?* [Blog post]. Accessed at https:// positivepsychology.com/self-efficacy/ on January 25, 2021.

Ainsworth, L. (2017, October 9). *The clarity problem—and the teacher solution!* [Blog post]. Accessed at www .larryainsworth.com/blog/the-clarity-problem-and-the-teacher-solution/ on May 25, 2020.

Alcala, L. (n.d.). *Highlighting mistakes: A grading strategy* [Video file]. Accessed at https://learn.teachingchannel .com/video/math-test-grading-tips on July 3, 2020.

Almarode, J., & Vandas, K. (2019). *Clarity for learning: Five essential practices that empower students and teachers.* Thousand Oaks, CA: Corwin Press.

Bandura, A. (1994). Self-efficacy. In V. S. Ramachandran (Ed.), *Encyclopedia of human behavior* (Vol. 4, pp. 71–81). New York: Academic Press. Accessed at www.uky.edu/~eushe2/Bandura/Bandura1994EHB.pdf on July 13, 2020.

Bandura, A. (Ed.). (1995). *Self-efficacy in changing societies.* New York: Cambridge University Press.

Bandura, A. (1997). *Self-efficacy: The exercise of control.* New York: Freeman.

Bandura, A. (2009). Cultivate self-efficacy for personal and organizational effectiveness. In E. A. Locke (Ed.), *Handbook of principles of organizational behavior: Indispensable knowledge for evidence based management* (2nd ed., pp. 179–200). West Sussex, England: John Wiley and Sons.

Bolman, L. G., & Deal, T. E. (2011). *Leading with soul: An uncommon journey of spirit* (3rd ed.). San Francisco: Jossey-Bass.

Broadfoot, P., Daugherty, R., Gardner, J., Gipps, C., Harlen, W., James, M., et al. (1999). *Assessment for learning: Beyond the black box.* London: Nuffield Foundation. Accessed at www.nuffieldfoundation.org/sites/default /files/files/beyond_blackbox.pdf on June 22, 2020.

Brookhart, S. M. (2012). Preventing feedback fizzle. *Educational Leadership, 70*(1), 24–29. Accessed at www.ascd .org/publications/educational-leadership/sept12/vol70/num01/Preventing-Feedback-Fizzle.aspx on July 14, 2020.

Brookhart, S. M. (2017). *How to give effective feedback to your students* (2nd ed). Alexandria, VA: Association for Supervision and Curriculum Development.

Brookover, W. B., & Lezotte, L. W. (1979). *Changes in school characteristics coincident with changes in student achievement.* East Lansing, MI: Institute for Research on Teaching. Accessed at http://education.msu.edu/irt /PDFs/OccasionalPapers/op017.pdf on July 6, 2020.

Brown, T. [ctimbrown]. (2020, June 24). And they begin disguising their struggles through behaviors that drive tchrs crazy. "See they don't even care". They do care, it's just how they present themselves because they see no pathway to success as they compare themselves to their classmates [Twitter moment]. Accessed at https:// twitter.com/ctimbrown/status/1275936350236299264 on June 27, 2020.

Campbell, D., & Sandino, T. (2019). *Sustaining corporate culture in a growing organization.* Cambridge, MA: Harvard Business School.

Cancellieri, P. (2020a, June 11). *Creating a culture of feedback book study: Session two—How am I doing?* [Video file]. Accessed at https://solutiontree.wistia.com/medias/ra3371pryg on June 27, 2020.

Cancellieri, P. (2020b, July 17). *What does "meaningful feedback to students" look like in a remote environment?* [Video file]. Presented at the Solution Tree Remote Teaching Virtual Institute, Bloomington, IN.

Chappuis, J. (2012). "How am I doing?" *Educational Leadership, 70*(1), 36–41. Accessed at www.ascd.org /publications/educational-leadership/sept12/vol70/num01/%C2%A3How-Am-I-Doing%C2%A2%C2%A3 .aspx on July 16, 2020.

Chappuis, J. (2015). *Seven strategies of assessment* for *learning.* New York: Pearson Education.

Chappuis, J., & Stiggins, R. (2020). *Classroom assessment* for *student learning: Doing it right—Using it well* (3rd ed.). Hoboken, NJ: Pearson Education.

Chappuis, J., Stiggins, R., Chappuis, S., & Arter, J. (2012). *Classroom assessment* for *student learning: Doing it right—Using it well.* (2nd ed). New York: Pearson Education.

Chappuis, S., Commodore, C., & Stiggins, R. (2016). *Balanced assessment systems: Leadership, quality and the role of classroom assessment.* Thousand Oaks, CA: Corwin Press.

Cognition Education. (2012, May 12). *Self-reported grades with John Hattie* [Video file]. Accessed at https://vimeo .com/41465488 on June 23, 2020.

Collins, J. (2001). *Good to great: Why some companies make the leap . . . and others don't.* New York: HarperCollins.

Conzemius, A. E., & O'Neill, J. (2014). *The handbook for SMART school teams: Revitalizing best practices for collaboration* (2nd ed.). Bloomington, IN: Solution Tree Press.

Crary, D. (2018, July 26). Girl Scouts fight membership decline with "girl power" messaging. *NECN Los Angeles.* Accessed at www.necn.com/news/national-international/girl-scouts-membership-decline-girl-power -messaging/2015535/ on February 14, 2021.

Donohoo, J. (2017, January 9). *Collective teacher efficacy: The effect size research and six enabling conditions* [Blog post]. Accessed at https://thelearningexchange.ca/collective-teacher-efficacy/ on October 29, 2020.

Duckworth, A. (2020, December 6). *Cultivating confidence: Succeeding one step at a time* [Blog post]. Accessed at https://characterlab.org/tips-of-the-week/cultivating-confidence/ on February 22, 2021.

DuFour, R., & DuFour, R. (2012). *The school leader's guide to Professional Learning Communities at Work.* Bloomington, IN: Solution Tree Press.

DuFour, R., DuFour, R., Eaker, R., Many, T. W., & Mattos, M. (2016). *Learning by doing: A handbook for Professional Learning Communities at Work* (3rd ed.). Bloomington, IN: Solution Tree Press.

DuFour, R., Eaker, R., & DuFour, R. (2007). *The power of Professional Learning Communities at Work: Bringing the big ideas to life.* Bloomington, IN: Solution Tree Press.

Dweck, C. S. (2016). *Mindset: The new psychology of success.* New York: Ballantine Books.

Feldman, D. L., Smith, A. T., & Waxman, B. L. (2017). *"Why we drop out": Understanding and disrupting student pathways to leaving school.* New York: Teachers College Press.

Ferriter, W. M. (2020). *The big book of tools for collaborative teams in a PLC at Work.* Bloomington, IN: Solution Tree Press.

Ferriter, W. M., & Cancellieri, P. J. (2017). *Creating a culture of feedback: Solutions for creating the learning spaces students deserve.* Bloomington, IN: Solution Tree Press.

Frey, N., Hattie, J., & Fisher, D. (2018). *Developing assessment-capable visible learners, grades K–12.* Thousand Oaks, CA: Corwin Press.

Fisher, D., & Frey, N. (2012). Making time for feedback. *Educational Leadership, 70*(1), 42–46.

Fuchs, D., Fuchs, L. S., Mathes, P. G., Lipsey, M. W., & Roberts, P. (2002). Is "learning disabilities" just a fancy term for low achievement? A meta-analysis of reading differences between low achievers with and without the label. In R. Bradley, L. Danielson, & D. P. Hallahan (Eds.), *Identification of learning disabilities: Research to practice— The LEA series on special education and disability* (pp. 737–762). Mahwah, NJ: Lawrence Erlbaum Associates.

Gobble, T., Onuscheck, M., Reibel, A. R., & Twadell, E. (2016). *Proficiency-based assessment: Process, not product.* Bloomington, IN: Solution Tree Press.

Goleman, D. (2005). *Emotional intelligence: Why it can matter more than IQ* (10th anniversary ed.). New York: Bantam Books.

Groysberg, B., Lee, J., Price, J., & Cheng, J. Y. L. (2018, January). The leader's guide to corporate culture. *Harvard Business Review.* Accessed at https://hbr.org/2018/01/the-leaders-guide-to-corporate-culture on February 14, 2021.

Guskey, T. R. (2019, June 27). *Grades versus comments: What does the research really tell us?* [Blog post]. Accessed at http://tguskey.com/grades-versus-comments-what-does-the-research-really-tell-us/ on February 18, 2021.

Hattie, J. (2009). *Visible learning: A synthesis of over 800 meta-analyses relating to achievement.* New York: Routledge.

Hattie, J. (2011). Feedback in schools. In R. M. Sutton, M. J. Hornsey, & K. M. Douglas (Eds.), *Feedback: The communication of praise, criticism and advice* (pp. 265–278). New York: Peter Lang.

Hattie, J. (2012). Know thy impact. *Educational Leadership, 70*(1), 18–23.

Hattie, J. (2017). *Visible Learning Plus: 250+ influences on student achievement* [Infographic]. Accessed at https://visible-learning.org/wp-content/uploads/2018/03/VLPLUS-252-Influences-Hattie-ranking-DEC-2017.pdf on July 29, 2019.

Hattie, J. (2018, May 1). *What is "collective teacher efficacy?"* [Video file]. Accessed at https://vimeo.com/267382804 on November 10, 2020.

Hattie, J., & Clarke, S. (2019). *Visible learning: Feedback.* New York: Routledge.

Heinonen, S. (2019, December 3). *Community organizations face declining membership.* Accessed at www.thereminder.com/localnews/greaterspringfield/community-organizations-face-declining-membership/ on February 14, 2021.

Illinois Report Card. (2020). *School snapshot: Adlai E. Stevenson High School.* Accessed at www.illinoisreportcard.com/School.aspx?schoolid=340491250130001 on February 21, 2021.

Jackson, Y. (2011). *The pedagogy of confidence: Inspiring high intellectual performance in urban schools.* New York: Teachers College Press.

Jakicic, C. (2017, May 22). *Are essential standards a part of the assessment process?* Accessed at http://allthingsassessment.info/2017/05/22/essential-standards-and-the-assessment-process/ on February 14, 2021.

Jeffrey, S. (2018, July 27). *How leaders use symbols to influence others.* Accessed at www.business2community.com/leadership/how-leaders-use-symbols-to-influence-others-02096894 on February 14, 2021.

Kanold, T. D. (2021). *SOUL! Fulfilling the promise of your professional life as a teacher and leader.* Bloomington, IN: Solution Tree Press.

Kerr, D., Hulen, T. A., Heller, J., & Butler, B. K. (2021). *What about us? The PLC at Work process for grades preK–2 teams.* Bloomington, IN: Solution Tree Press.

Lipnevich, A. A., & Smith, J. K. (2008). *Response to assessment feedback: The effects of grades, praise, and source of information.* Princeton, NJ: Educational Testing Service. Accessed at www.drivelearning.org/uploads/4/4/1/1 /44110523/response_to_assessment_feedback.pdf on January 25, 2021.

Long, C. (2017, December 19). Some of the surprising reasons why students drop out of school. *NEA Today.* Accessed at http://neatoday.org/2017/12/19/why-students-drop-out-of-school/ on July 3, 2020.

Love, N. B., Stiles, K. E., Mundry, S. E., & DiRanna, K. (2008). *The data coach's guide to improving learning for all students: Unleashing the power of collaborative inquiry.* Thousand Oaks, CA: Corwin Press.

Marzano, R. J. (2007). *The art and science of teaching: A comprehensive framework for effective instruction.* Alexandria, VA: Association for Supervision and Curriculum Development.

Marzano, R. J. (2017). *The new art and science of teaching.* Bloomington, IN: Solution Tree Press.

Marzano, R. J., Pickering, D. J., & Heflebower, T. (2011). *The highly engaged classroom.* Bloomington, IN: Marzano Research.

McLeod, S. A. (2018). *The preoperational stage of cognitive development.* Accessed at www.simplypsychology.org /preoperational.html on February 1, 2020.

Moss, C. M., & Brookhart, S. M. (2019). *Advancing formative assessment in every classroom: A guide for instructional leaders* (2nd ed.). Alexandria, VA: Association for Supervision and Curriculum Development.

Muhammad, A. (2017). *Transforming school culture: How to overcome staff division* (2nd ed.). Bloomington, IN: Solution Tree Press.

Newby, L., & Sallee, J. (2011, Winter). 4-H membership recruitment/retention problems: A meta-analysis of possible causes and solutions. *Journal of Youth Development, 6*(4). Accessed at https://core.ac.uk/download /pdf/205515613.pdf on February 14, 2021.

Organisation for Economic Co-operation and Development. (2008). *Assessment for learning: Formative assessment.* Paris: Author. Accessed at www.oecd.org/site/educeri21st/40600533.pdf on June 23, 2020.

Ormrod, J. E. (2008). *Human learning* (5th ed.). Upper Saddle River, NJ: Pearson.

Pajares, F. (1997). Current directions in self-efficacy research. In M. Maehr & P. R. Pintrich (Eds.), *Advances in motivation and achievement* (Vol. 10, pp. 1–49). Greenwich, CT: JAI Press.

Pink, D. H. (2009). *Drive: The surprising truth about what motivates us.* New York: Riverhead Books.

Roberts, M. (2019). *Enriching the learning: Meaningful extensions for proficient students in a PLC at Work.* Bloomington, IN: Solution Tree Press.

Ruiz-Primo, M. A., & Brookhart, S. M. (2018). *Using feedback to improve learning.* New York: Routledge.

Sadler, D. R. (1989). Formative assessment and the design of instructional systems. *Instructional Science, 18,* 119–144.

Sadler, D. R. (1998). Formative assessment: Revisiting the territory. *Assessment in Education, 5*(1), 77–84.

Schinske, J., & Tanner, K. (2014, Summer). Teaching more by grading less (or differently). *CBE Life Sciences Education, 13*(2). Accessed at www.ncbi.nlm.nih.gov/pmc/articles/PMC4041495/ on February 18, 2021.

Schmidt, S., & Epstein, K. (2019, September 11). Lawsuits. Possible bankruptcy. Declining numbers. Is there a future for the Boy Scouts? *The Washington Post.* Accessed at www.washingtonpost.com/local/social-issues /lawsuits-possible-bankruptcy-declining-members-is-there-a-future-for-the-boy-scouts/2019/09/11/54699d6a -ce53-11e9-8c1c-7c8ee785b855_story.html on February 14, 2021.

Shute, V. J. (2007). *Focus on formative feedback.* Princeton, NJ: Educational Testing Service. Accessed at https:// www.ets.org/Media/Research/pdf/RR-07-11.pdf on January 25, 2021.

Stiggins, R. J., Arter, J. A., Chappuis, J., & Chappuis, S. (2007). *Classroom assessment for student learning: Doing it right—Using it well.* Upper Saddle River, NJ: Pearson Education.

Stiggins, R., & Chappuis, J. (2005). Using student-involved classroom assessment to close achievement gaps. *Theory Into Practice, 44*(1), 11–18.

Taylor, B. (2017, June 1). 5 questions to ask about corporate culture to get beyond the usual meaningless blather. *Harvard Business Review*. Accessed at https://hbr.org/2017/06/5-questions-to-ask-about-corporate -culture-to-get-beyond-the-usual-meaningless-blather on February 14, 2021.

TEDx Talks. (2013, November 22). *Why are so many of our teachers and schools so successful? John Hattie at TEDxNorrköping* [Video file]. Accessed at www.youtube.com/watch?v=rzwJXUieD0U on June 27, 2020.

Tomlinson, C. A. (2015, January 27). Differentiation does, in fact, work. *Education Week*. Accessed at www .edweek.org/ew/articles/2015/01/28/differentiation-does-in-fact-work.html on January 2, 2020.

U.S. News and World Report. (2021). *Best high schools rankings: Adlai E Stevenson High School*. Accessed at www .usnews.com/education/best-high-schools/illinois/districts/adlai-e-stevenson-hsd-125/adlai-e-stevenson-high -school-6955 on February 21, 2021.

Van Horn, S. (2014, November 7). *Working on weekly class SMART goals* [Blog post]. Accessed at www .3rdgradethoughts.com/2014/11/working-on-weekly-class-smart-goals.html on June 28, 2020.

Visible Learning. [visiblelearning]. (2018, October 8). "@john_hattie is still updating his research involving 1500+ meta-analyses and 300+ million students, but the story remains the same. Check out the new and updated chart of the #Visiblelearning 250+ influences on student achievement. http://ow.ly/inK450jmj9r" [Twitter moment]. Accessed at https://twitter.com/VisibleLearning/status/1049460717873782791on February 19, 2021.

Watkins, M. D. (2013, May 15). What is organizational culture? And why should we care? *Harvard Business Review*. Accessed at https://hbr.org/2013/05/what-is-organizational-culture on February 8, 2020.

Williams, K. C., & Hierck, T. (2015). *Starting a movement: Building culture from the inside out in professional learning communities*. Bloomington, IN: Solution Tree Press.

Wiggins, G. (2012). Seven keys to effective feedback. *Educational Leadership, 70*(1). Accessed at www.ascd.org /publications/educational-leadership/sept12/vol70/num01/Seven-Keys-to-Effective-Feedback.aspx on February 18, 2021.

Wiliam, D. (2011). *Embedded formative assessment*. Bloomington, IN: Solution Tree Press.

Wiliam, D. (2012). Feedback: Part of a system. *Educational Leadership, 70*(1), 30–34.

Wiliam, D. [dylanwiliam]. (2015, November 22). Or, to put it another way, "Make feedback into detective work" [Twitter moment]. Accessed at https://twitter.com/dylanwiliam/ status/668635191531958272 on June 27, 2020.

Wiliam, D. (2016). The secret of effective feedback. *Educational Leadership, 73*(7). Accessed at www.ascd.org /publications/educational-leadership/apr16/vol73/num07/The-Secret-of-Effective-Feedback.aspx on July 14, 2020.

Wolf, G. (2007, November 12). *What is self-efficacy?* [Blog post]. Accessed at https://quantifiedself.com/blog/what -is-selfefficacy/ on November 10, 2020.

INDEX

Learning by Doing, Third Edition
Richard DuFour, Rebecca DuFour, Robert Eaker, Thomas W. Many, and Mike Mattos
Discover how to close the knowing-doing gap and transform your school or district into a high-performing PLC. The powerful third edition of this comprehensive action guide updates and expands on new and significant PLC topics. Explore fresh strategies, tools, and tips for hiring and retaining new staff, creating team-developed common formative assessments, implementing systematic interventions, and more.
BKF746

Concise Answers to Frequently Asked Questions About Professional Learning Communities at Work®
Mike Mattos, Richard DuFour, Rebecca DuFour, Robert Eaker, and Thomas W. Many
Get all of your PLC questions answered. Designed as a companion resource to *Learning by Doing: A Handbook for Professional Learning Communities at Work®* (3rd ed.), this powerful, quick-reference guidebook is a must-have for teachers and administrators working to create and sustain the PLC process. You and your team will turn to this invaluable reference tool again and again as questions and complications arise along your PLC journey.
BKF705

Personalized Learning in a PLC at Work®
Timothy Stuart, Sascha Heckmann, Mike Mattos, and Austin Buffum
Highly effective learning-progressive schools share two common elements: they operate as high-functioning PLCs with well-implemented RTI structures, and they promote student agency in the learning process. Rely on this resource to help you build a highly effective school where students are engaged in personalized learning experiences and empowered to take ownership of the four critical questions of the PLC at Work® process.
BKF703

The Big Book of Tools for Collaborative Teams in a PLC at Work®
William M. Ferriter
Build your team's capacity to become agents of positive change. Organized around the four critical questions of a PLC at Work®, this comprehensive book of field-tested, easy-to-use tools provides an explicit structure for collaborative teams. Rely on these resources and best practices to help you establish team norms, navigate common challenges, develop collective teacher efficacy, and more.
BKF898

Creating a Culture of Feedback
William M. Ferriter and Paul J. Cancellieri
Because of the importance placed on high-stakes evaluations, schools have built cultures that greatly emphasize grading. In this book, the authors urge educators to shift their classroom focus, prioritizing effective feedback over grades. Discover how to state learning intentions clearly and provide individualized feedback to give students all the information they need to succeed.
BKF731

Solution Tree | Press *a division of* Solution Tree

Visit SolutionTree.com or call 800.733.6786 to order.

"Tremendous, tremendous, tremendous!

The speaker made me do some very deep internal reflection about the **PLC process** and the personal responsibility I have in making the school improvement process work **for ALL kids.**"

—Marc Rodriguez, teacher effectiveness coach,
Denver Public Schools, Colorado

PD Services

Our experts draw from decades of research and their own experiences to bring you practical strategies for building and sustaining a high-performing PLC. You can choose from a range of customizable services, from a one-day overview to a multiyear process.

Book your PLC PD today!
888.763.9045

Solution Tree